YOUR CHILD DESERVES A HEAD START!

A modern, practical method of developing your child's potentials.

HOW TO TEACH YOUR CHILD TO ENJOY SCHOOL

HOW TO HELP YOUR CHILD GROW EMOTIONALLY

HOW TO COMMUNICATE WITH CHILDREN

HOW TO HELP YOUR CHILD DEVELOP A GOOD MEMORY

And much, much more in Clyde M. Narramore's

UNDERSTANDING YOUR CHILDREN

Including Two National Bestsellers:

How to Understand and Influence Children

How to Tell Your Children About Sex

UNDERSTANDING YOUR CHILDREN

Clyde M. Narramore, Ed.D.

Including:

How to Understand and Influence Children

How to Tell Your Children About Sex

ZONDERVAN
PUBLISHING HOUSE
OF THE ZONDERVAN CORPORATION | GRAND RAPIDS. MICHIGAN 49506

UNDERSTANDING YOUR CHILDREN

A ZONDERVAN BOOK
Published by Pyramid Publications, Inc. for
Zondervan Publishing House

HOW TO UNDERSTAND AND INFLUENCE CHILDREN
Zondervan Publishing House edition published 1957
Ninth printing 1967

Copyright © 1957 by Clyde M. Narramore

HOW TO TELL YOUR CHILDREN ABOUT SEX
Zondervan Publishing House edition published June 1958
Twelfth printing October 1967

Copyright © 1958 by Clyde M. Narramore

Zondervan Books edition published March 1969
Third printing April 1972
Fourth printing 1973

ZONDERVAN BOOKS are published by Zondervan Publishing
House, 1415 Lake Drive, S.E., Grand Rapids, Michigan
49506, U.S.A.

If, in instructing a child, you are vexed with it for want of adroitness, try, if you have never tried before, to write with your left hand, and then remember that a child is all left hand.

—J. F. BOYSE

Yes, teachers belong to a great company— the company of the Lord Jesus Christ, as well as Socrates, Plato and Aristotle; of Abelard and St. Thomas; of Rousseau, Pestalozzi and Froebel; of Horace Mann and William James. Ours is a vital work for into our keeping is placed the destiny of nations!

—AUTHOR UNKNOWN

CONTENTS

CHAPTER ONE

Teaching and Learning

PARENTS AND TEACHERS

Mrs. LANE, a primary teacher, had just rearranged the last small chair and picked up the last bit of crumpled paper from the floor when the Sunday school superintendent stepped in the doorway and said, "You sure had your hands full this morning with four new ones, didn't you?"

"Yes," she answered, "but I love it! I'd rather teach children than do anything else in the world. Once you've had the thrill of seeing bright little eyes hang onto every word you say, you forget about all the preparation and cleaning up that goes with it."

How right she was! The delight of teaching is one of our greatest satisfactions in life. This interchange of knowledge is one of the characteristics which distinguishes man from the animal kingdom. It is a God-given difference. The Almighty created men and women, boys and girls, to think, to perceive the truth, to make decisions. It is a pleasure to teach because human beings are not completely happy unless they are learning.

It is especially true that children love to learn. Unless this intellectual need is met they feel frustrated. As they gain knowledge, their personalities develop. They are both happier and healthier when learning.

A mother and father cannot avoid the role of a teacher. Parents teach by what they say, what they do and what they don't do. When they are conscious of this important role, they can guide young feet into vast realms of knowledge. A trip to the zoo . . . the gift of a well-selected book . . . family worship time . . . all are teaching occasions.

All teaching, however, is not done in the home. We find it done in public schools, through private lessons, in Christian day schools, and by the church school. Here the volunteer finds that helping children to learn is one of his greatest joys. It is one way you can invest yourself in the service of the Lord and in other people. As you teach children your ideas and ideals live on. They, in time, teach others and so your ideas continue from generation to generation. A boy or a girl is a bank in which the teacher or parent deposits his ideals.

Effective teaching is not accidental. It is a science. Whether you study the process scientifically or learn these principles by experience, you will see that good teaching and learning follow basic principles. It is easier if you know how people actually learn.

The principles discussed in this section of *How to Understand and Influence Children* are ones that man has learned about himself. As you learn and follow them, whether you are a parent or a teacher, you will become a more successful guide of boys and girls.

MIND OR MUSCLE

I was a six-year-old embryonic psychologist when I overheard my older brother talking with mother about school. He had just enrolled in high school. She asked, "Son, what courses are you taking?"

Proudly my brother began to list the subjects for which he had signed up. The last one he named was "algebra."

"Algebra?" she questioned. "Why are you taking algebra?"

"Because they told me that algebra would train my mind."

As a little first-grader, I supposed that my brother was right. I believed that it was possible to train the mind like we train a muscle. Wouldn't it be wonderful if the mind *were* a muscle! Then all you would have to do would be to train it. Once the mind was fully exercised

You can't train the mind like a muscle.

and developed it would automatically be able to solve all problems.

But the mind is not a muscle. About all one learns from the study of algebra is algebra! It is impossible to sharpen the mind in one subject and expect it to do clever work in all others.

True, each thing you learn may have connections with other bits of information, but each has its own setting and must be mastered individually. This is one of the reasons why it is possible for a person to attend church regularly and not necessarily relate his worship experience to his Monday through Saturday ethics. The instructor must show the pupil how to relate Bible knowledge to everyday living.

So teaching is here to stay. There will always be another lesson to learn, another subject to master. And as the teacher acquires better and more effective ways of teaching, he can more successfully help the pupil continue the learning process.

APPEAL AND APPEARANCE

Children have confidence in parents and teachers who are well-groomed.

"Be sure to look in the mirror twice before you leave home Sunday mornings," advised a Sunday school superintendent at a teachers' meeting.

And he was right. He

11

knew that many teachers, and also parents, handicap themselves in their relationship to children by neglecting their appearance.

Children lose their respect for a father who "lays down the law" and yet who has a sloppy appearance, or a mother who mopes around the house in a soiled housecoat with half-combed hair. Cleanliness generates respect. Dad, in a clean sport shirt, can talk more convincingly of the need of clean sportsmanship in life. And Mom, in a clean print dress makes home more appealing to the restless child.

Teachers, too, handicap themselves when they pay too little attention to their appearance and bearing. A truly spiritual person in a somber dress may be unnoticed, while someone with a flare for smart appearance and less spirituality attracts the children. Naturally, the ideal is a combination of the two.

It is only natural for children to have confidence in adults who have respect for their own appearance. The child does not see the inside. He sees the outside, and being attracted to a well-groomed person, he listens to what that person says. When you look twice at yourself, he looks twice at you, and listens to what you say about the Lord.

Whatever you wear, it should be clean and pressed. Form your own check list. How about the following:

1. Is my collar clean?
2. Are my shirt cuffs clean?
3. Are there any spots on my tie?
4. Is my suit, or dress, well-pressed?
5. Is my suit brushed?
6. Have I worn this dress every Sunday for the last six months?
7. Are my shoes polished, or my white shoes clean?
8. Are my heels run over?
9. Are there holes in my socks or runs in my stockings?
10. Are my seams straight?
11. Is my hair well groomed?
12. Are my nails clean?
13. Are my teeth clean and is my breath sweet?

14. Have I asked my best friend if I have B.O.?
15. Am I appropriately dressed?

ALIVE AND ALERT

Both Tom Rawlston and Peggy Palmer were acknowledged to be good Sunday school teachers. Yet both were

Often, the difference between a successful person and an unsuccessful one is a vital personality!

entirely different. Tom was a big, husky fellow, six feet, two, weighing 195, while Peggy was small and slight, known to weigh 105 once, when her clothes were wringing wet. Tom blustered. Peggy spoke in a low voice. But both had one quality in common. They were alive and alert.

The difference, not only between unsuccessful and successful teachers, but persons, is often this—a vital personality. Good leaders, and all good teachers are dynamic! They speak distinctly and expressively, making the stories they tell alive. They use short punchy sentences. They use dialogue and they raise questions. They give the children opportunities to express themselves. They are vitally interested in their contributions, however trivial they seem to the adult. Their enthusiasm and zeal for living shines through everything they do.

Vitality can be developed. It has no relationship to your age. True, there are differences in people. Some are the "bubbling" type . . . some are not. To one it is easy to "effervesce" . . . others must make an effort. But you can improve your "zeal appeal." And when you realize how

13

important it is to yourself, as well as to your teaching, you will.

Health, naturally, comes first. In this day of vitamin pills and check-ups, you can maintain your health at top peak. See to it that you give yourself the advantages of all our modern physical help.

Then you are ready for other kinds of help. You can take different courses, in night school if you live in a city or by correspondence if you live in a smaller town or country. All knowledge adds to your alertness. True, you may discard some of the things suggested as too extreme, but the basic facts will be helpful. How about a course in public speaking? It will make you more interesting and help you gain confidence. Perhaps a course in public relations or psychology, learning a few fundamentals of human relationships, is available to you. Be up on things. Read a lot. All these will help to build up your sparkle.

Another way to help yourself is to check over your ideas, and sort out your critical negative ones. You drive children away from you when you speak disparagingly of them, as delinquents or as young hoodlums. Think, rather, of their alert faces and bright little ways, and your happy thoughts will reflect in your face and voice.

Probably the best way to come alive is to love others and show it. If you listen when children talk of their doings, your face will naturally glow. If you visit their homes, they know you care. An occasional pat on the back and an affectionate "nickname" does as much for you as it does for the children.

You don't need money, or "looks" or much formal education. But you do need to be alive!

PREPARED OR PERPLEXED

One of the biggest jobs in the world is this: shaping a life. Parents and Sunday school teachers who have this important vision do not regret the time and energy involved in working effectively with boys and girls.

Nothing takes the place of preparation.

If you are not devoting much time to preparing your Sunday school lessons, you probably do not have a vision of the true importance of your work. Many teachers have solved this problem by praying—asking God to work in their hearts. When God does show you the importance of teaching children, you will rearrange your schedule so that you will have time to make adequate preparation each week.

Nothing can take the place of preparation. The teacher who comes to class without sufficient preparation is constantly trying to keep ahead of the children. But the well-prepared teacher meets emergencies more easily. She is relaxed and poised.

"I find it doesn't take any more time," said one teacher, "to prepare ahead, and yet it gives me an opportunity during the week to think of what I'm going to teach. Extra ideas come into my mind and keep the lessons from being ordinary."

A simple plan will help you prepare ahead. For instance:

Sunday afternoon: Read the Bible lesson you are to teach the following Sunday.

Monday: Study the lesson quarterly.

Wednesday: Discuss the lesson with a member of the family or a friend.

Thursday: Prepare an object lesson or flannelgraph figures.

Friday: Phone the absentees and encourage them to come next Sunday.

Saturday: Give your entire lesson a final check, and get your objects and other materials ready to take Sunday morning.

When what you have to teach is a part of you, a dozen squirming children and two dozen interruptions will not interrupt your train of thought.

ATMOSPHERE AND ATTITUDE

How often have you gone into a room and said to yourself, "My, I like it in here!"

The atmosphere of the room has a definite effect on people. In fact, everyone is becoming more and more conscious of his surroundings. Whether in a restaurant, office, department store, home or Sunday school, the human mind and body respond sensitively to the environment. Colors, lighting, pictures on the wall, and a host of other factors affect our frame of mind and our behavior.

The atmosphere of a room has a definite effect on how children act and learn.

As a consulting psychologist in schools, I have visited many classrooms. It is interesting to "feel" the room atmosphere created by walls, furniture, color, displays, draperies, temperature, plants and many other things.

Each room in the home, each classroom in the church has its own atmosphere. The wise parent or teacher asks himself, "Does the arrangement of this room command the respect of the children? Does it predispose the child to do his best? To learn?"

If the answer is "no," the normal reaction will be to wish for a new home or new church. However, a new building isn't necessarily the answer. Imagination is! What can you do about your home or your teaching space?

Naturally, in your home you have many opportunities for improvement. By keeping your eyes open and by reading, you can learn how to create this desirable atmosphere.

At church, you are limited by the space allotted to you. However, even if your teaching area is not ideal, you can still make it attractive. The first step is to remove the old charts, verses and notices which seem to collect in most churches. Then put up attractive posters and items that have meaning for your children. And each Sunday before class time see that the chairs and whatever else you use, are in place. Flower arrangements, missionary pictures, class photographs and an attractive Scripture verse can do much to improve the teaching atmosphere. An attractive Bible arranged appropriately can do much to create an atmosphere conducive to worshiping God and learning about Him.

The class that has its own room is fortunate. Clean, attractive drapes can be your first project. Perhaps the class can have a Saturday "improvement session," cleaning and polishing the chairs or doing whatever the children and parents can to make their room a nicer place to be together in on Sundays.

In an attractive room discipline problems are usually considerably less. The child's spirit will grow receptive and he is now in an environment in which you can teach him the Word and the things of Christ.

HALE AND HEARTY

Don was a husky eight-year-old, who had never done well in school, yet tests indicated that he was a little above average in intelligence. His Sunday school teacher couldn't understand why. She was puzzled. She tried different ways of stimulating his interest. There was little response. Finally, she went to his parents and questioned them about his health. They assured the teacher that Don was in "perfect health." Even so, her questioning alerted them, and Don was given a physical examination.

The examination proved what was the matter with Don. He was a glandular case, definitely in need of

Children with behavior and achievement problems very often have health problems.

medical care. A few months of medical attention made Don a "new boy" with a new interest in both public school and Sunday school.

Don, like many children, was hindered by a physical problem. In fact, a study of several thousand low-achieving school children in a metropolitan area revealed that the vast majority were not in top physical condition.

School psychologists who make case studies of children with special behavior and achievement problems know that many of them have related physical problems such as brain damage, glandular malfunctions, low vitality and other health handicaps. A child's ability to learn is directly related to his health.

Poor health keeps children from concentrating. It robs them of well directed energy. It subjects them to easy distraction. Poor health also makes children discouraged so that they have no real incentive to learn. Boys and girls who are considered lazy or "ornery" are often children with health problems, in need of medical and psychological attention.

Every parent and teacher has a definite responsibility to observe children with a view of detecting those who have physical problems. Parents should see that their children have periodic health examinations. And teachers should consider their responsibility for "spotting" boys and girls who might possibly have health problems. A healthy child is an alert child!

SUITABLE AND SELECTIVE

Three mothers were shopping together. One bought size six, another size eight, and the third size ten. They all bought different sizes because their children were of different ages. They didn't give the matter a second thought. They knew that different-sized children had to have different-sized clothes.

The same is true of lessons. Not long ago specialists in child growth and development became concerned about the appropriateness of what was taught to a child. It was called "psychological fitting."

If your lessons don't fit psychologically, the children won't wear them.

"Look," they said, "children aren't little adults. At six years of age they generally have certain physical, intellectual, social and emotional development. But at eight, most boys and girls have reached a very different level of interest and understanding. This means that you must suit a different curriculum and approach to each age level."

This was important news to parents and teachers. But it didn't really take hold until recently. You see, it meant many things. For example, it meant that a junior church might be more appropriate for young boys and girls than the adult church. It meant that publishers of Sunday school material should consult scientific studies about growth and development in order to make their literature best suited to each age level. It meant that all teacher training should be centered around what fits, and what doesn't fit children.

You can make sure that your material, illustrations, and techniques are appropriate for your children by ordering literature from outstanding evangelical Sunday school publishers. They have psychology and curriculum specialists on their staff who see to it that all their material is geared to each age level.

Here's another suggestion: review the child growth and development information presented in this book. It will help you get through to the children you are trying to reach. And teaching will be easier. Yes, the authority was right who said, "If your lessons don't fit psychologically, the kids just won't wear them."

DAYDREAMS AND DISTRACTIONS

Kathryn was a little girl who couldn't sit still and concentrate for ten seconds on anything. The teacher wondered why. A visit to the home proved that Kathryn was troubled. The father and mother were separated. The mother was struggling to achieve success as a singer and had little time for her daughter. In Kathryn's case both parents were too self-centered to make changes for the betterment of their child. The teacher gave Kathryn love and attention, something she did not know at home, and in time was able to help her.

This case pointed up the truth that there is a reason behind a child's inattention. Perhaps it is physical, as we discussed in the previous section of this chapter. But it may be caused by a mental disturbance.

Emotional disturbances show up in various ways in children (and adults). Some youngsters reveal their inner tensions by not paying attention. The least little distraction takes them away from what they are trying to learn. Others are "forgetters." They seem to have to be told over and over again, and

A child who is preoccupied with inner conflicts needs your special help.

even then it may not "sink in." Still others escape the realities of conflict by day-dreaming. In fact, they spend almost as much time in another world as they do in their real one. Some children with emotional conflicts may try to resolve their feelings by hitting and shoving playmates or by blaming their brothers and sisters.

Regardless of the form taken, types of behavior are the child's way of trying to tell you that something is wrong, that things in his life are so disturbing that he cannot dismiss them. In other words, he can't get away from them long enough to give his full attention to learning.

Fortunately, there is help for such a child! The very fact that Christian parents and teachers understand these outward types of behavior as merely signs of inward trouble, makes them more patient.

In seeking the solution, it would be fine if there were Christian psychologists to whom these children could be referred. Of course, that's not always possible and perhaps not necessary. Lack of attention due to emotional conflicts is not something which must be handled solely by clinicians. All youngsters have some conflicts at times. So, you see, this maladjustment is not something so very different from what all other children experience. It differs principally in quantity, in its frequency and seriousness.

One of the best ways to help a child of average intelligence who is preoccupied with emotional conflicts, is *to see to it that he is not placed under more pressure.* Insisting that he be quiet, scolding him, forcing him to sit still and threatening him, only make the pressure greater. You still haven't reached the cause of his trouble. True, you may be able to force him to sit quietly for a few minutes, but he will still have his problem and will manifest it in other ways—perhaps by biting his nails, pulling his hair, wetting his clothes, stuttering, vomiting, complaining of headaches or seriously withdrawing so that he is even harder to reach.

Here is a technique that is nearly always successful: draw him out. Encourage him to talk. The chances are good that he will soon start talking about the things that bother him. As he has an opportunity to bring his conflicts and fears out into the open, to examine them and talk them, he may see some solutions or recognize his problem as being relatively unimportant. And of course, merely sharing them verbally with another person brings some release.

Drawing a child out doesn't mean "pumping" him Rather, it suggests that you relax with the child and arrange circumstances so that he can feel free to empty himself of his strong feelings. To do this, let the child do most of the talking. You should restate just enough of what he says so that he will be encouraged to say more. For example, if he says, "I hate everybody," you might say, "You feel, don't you, Jim, that you don't have any friends." Your job is not to censure or exclaim, but to patiently help him to express his feelings.

Remember, too, your pauses will reward you richly. When Jim stops talking for a moment or so, just wait until he starts again. These pauses may seem like "eternities" to you, but they are necessary when you are encouraging a disturbed child to "talk through" his conflicts. The more you use this technique of reflective counseling, the more skilled you will become and God will greatly bless your efforts.

If an upset child is trying to resolve his conflicts by aggression, provide him with more satisfactory ways of using his energy. It may surprise you how giving a little responsibility may help. One children's worker had gratifying results by appointing one boy in charge of getting a box to carry lunches to a picnic, another to carry the volley ball to the car and still another to carry the volley ball back. Responsibilities that require considerable body movement are always helpful. This is such an easy technique for parents and teachers to use—and it's very effective.

Here's another suggestion: Encourage the child by the fact that you are interested and that it will all work out. Give him a well-selected verse of Scripture that encourages him to talk to the Lord about the problem, because God is more interested than anyone in the world. Some verses you might suggest are, "Let the little children come unto me, and forbid them not" (Mark 10:14) or "Him that cometh to me I will in no wise cast out" (John 6:37). Surely, God never turns down *any* child—or adult!

Occasionally you will find a child who is so profoundly disturbed that he needs specialized professional help. Even the finest teacher does not have the professional competence to adequately help such a youngster. In such cases you will be wise to make proper referral. A Christian psychologist or psychiatrist is, of course, one of the best people to consult. But if a Christian is not available, the child will undoubtedly benefit from the diagnosis and therapy that a non-Christian can offer. Deeply disturbed children are actually suffering from mental illness; they need professional help as much as those who suffer from physical ailments!

These, then, are some of the ways you can help children who "have their minds on other things." Such boys and girls will take *much* of your time and *all* of your patience. But your efforts will be richly rewarded. Like other children, they have souls that will live somewhere forever. And whether they are won for Jesus Christ depends mostly on you—their parent or teacher!

VARIED AND VITAL

Use a variety of approaches when you work with children. It's more effective—and fun.

Coins, lilies, corn, wells. Christ Himself used these and many other objects and approaches when He taught the people. He employed illustrations. He frequently raised questions. He told stories. Once, He even wrote on the ground. And many times He simply sat with His disciples and quietly talked with them.

The effective teacher needs to follow the Master in His

teaching presentations. He will need to use every possible teaching device because each youngster is unique and has his own ways of learning. Some seem to grasp more quickly through visual presentation. Others through hearing. Children learn especially fast through active participation. But regardless of the approach, all children need things presented in a variety of ways.

God has given us five direct senses: hearing, seeing, tasting, smelling and feeling. Each of these is an avenue of learning. Unfortunately there is a tendency to use only one of these avenues—hearing. Most parents and teachers have overworked this listening approach. In fact, there are some boys and girls who have developed a measure of psychological deafness. Such inability or refusal to hear, may stem from constant, disagreeable impressions received through the ears—unpleasant sounds such as nagging, scolding, or other negative "talking." The human mind seems to protect itself from excessive talking and other sounds by shutting them out.

What has this to do with teaching? Just this: Most of the children you teach are not psychologically deaf, but they are conditioned against "talking." Therefore, you should emphasize a variety of presentations other than just the "listening" approach.

During the week when you are considering how you might present Sunday's lesson, you should ask yourself, "How many ways can I present this?" You may want to use a song, tell a story, use objects, have a class discussion, ask the children to build something that is related, or help them to dramatize it. As you use your imagination, you will find countless ways to present your lesson.

Teach by sight. Pictures can be brought to your class. There are countless applications. Biblical pictures of modern Palestine, those of children, or others illustrating the truth of the lesson. Simple maps can be used to give background and interest. Flannelgraphs fascinate any age. They can be simplified for the very young or beautifully drawn for adults. Of course films and film strips are always effective.

Teach by taste. Bring to class actual objects mentioned

in the Bible. Salt may be used to illustrate the verse: "Let your speech be always with grace, seasoned with salt" (Col. 4:6).

Teach by smell. This can be done by bringing a bottle of perfume, cologne or incense to illustrate "For we are unto God a sweet savour of Christ ..." (II Cor. 2:15). When your class sees how the fragrance permeates the room, they will understand how their Christian witness is noticed.

Teach by touch. Bring a rough cross and a few spikes to class. Let the children touch them when discussing the nailing of the Lord Jesus to the cross. Help them to realize that the incident was not merely a story which they are hearing but one which the Lord lived.

After you have used a variety of avenues to reach children, you will see how very effective they are. What's more, you'll get a new enjoyment out of teaching!

INSIGHTS AND IDEAS

"Children aren't taught: children learn."

"Children learn by repetition."

Undoubtedly you have heard both of these maxims many times. The one states a psychological truth that teachers are responsible for arranging learning experiences, but the child, himself, must gain the insights. The second statement emphasizes that knowledge is gained by the constant repetition of a fact.

Drill and review are important, but insight precedes them both.

You have wondered, perhaps, which one was true. The answer is simple—both. Drill and review do have an important place in the science of learning, but insight precedes them both.

Until a youngster understands or "catches on," drill and review are useless. In fact, they discourage a child from trying to learn at a later date.

Skilled teachers make certain that children definitely understand before they introduce drill. We all know youngsters who have drilled and drilled before they actually understood what they were drilling. Remember those piano lessons? You had almost no insight into the chords and sequences you were playing but you drilled on them just the same. Naturally, you kept making mistakes. Had your teacher, however, taken more time to explain thoroughly the principles involved, you would have gained a great deal from your practicing.

This concept is also true in memorizing Scripture. You can finally get children to parrot sounds that may be recognized as Bible verses, but you do them an injustice unless you take sufficient time to explain the meaning of the verses. After they have "gotten the idea," each verse is ready to be repeated and reviewed until it is committed to memory. There is hardly anything more important than Scripture memorization, and it behooves parents and teachers to use scientific methods to accomplish it.

The very fact that a child may be able to pronounce a word does not mean that he understands it. Here, for instance, is a list of words from one of our widely sung hymns: ascribe, throng, prostrate, ransomed, kindred, diadem and grace. How many of these does the child you are teaching understand? Try this list: sovereign, eternity, incarnate, stayed, reign, adore; or these: worship, Ancient of Days, pavilioned, girded, canopy, chariot, bountiful, descends, distills, frail. These words are all selected from the familiar hymns: *All Hail the Power of Jesus' Name, Come Thou Almighty King,* and *O, Worship the King.* Do not expect the child to enjoy singing such words without explaining their meaning. No wonder the boy from Brooklyn sang, "We shall come from Joisey bringing in the sheets!"

Keep asking yourself, "Does he understand? What evidence is there that he has gained this insight? Is he able to answer questions about it?" When you have mastered the skill of making sure that children understand before they drill and review, you will have attained a real measure of satisfaction in teaching, and besides, you will be using the limited time to best advantage.

ABSTRACT OR ACTUAL

"Whenever possible, let the children *rub* the curriculum," said an educator speaking at a teacher's workshop.

The "touch and learn" method is especially effective.

By that he meant that the closer boys and girls get to what they are studying, the more likely they are to learn, and learn well. This holds true in both the school and home classroom.

Learning through direct, first-hand experience is called concrete learning, as contrasted to abstract learning. For example, writing a number on the blackboard is an abstract approach. Marks on the board (numbers and symbols) merely represent amounts and directions. But touching, seeing and counting three pennies, then two additional pennies, is a concrete way of learning that three plus two equal five. That's because definite objects are involved.

When real objects are not available you can use a concrete approach by showing or making drawings and models. For example, if you can't buy a real Biblical water pitcher, you can help the children make similar ones or draw pictures of them. And the map of Palestine is one of the easiest to draw. The coast is a slanting line with two "humps" in it, and just opposite are "loops" for the Lake of Galilee and the Dead Sea. An excellent map can be made of salt, water, flour, bits of newspaper, food coloring, paste and a little essence of clove to give a pleasant odor.

This "touch and learn" approach is very effective because it stimulates and captivates the child's interest. Kinesthetic (muscle sense) learning has long been known to be exceptionally impressive. Yet, some unthinking teachers and harried mothers go along year after year, "talking" or "nagging" the lesson, without permitting their pupils to "rub the curriculum."

During your lesson preparation, ask yourself these questions, "What can I do to make this lesson specific and concrete?" "How can I let my pupils make, touch or see the objects included in this lesson?" or "How can I bridge the gap between talking about it and feeling it?" Or as a parent, ask yourself, "How can I teach Tommy the value of the money he spends?" "How can I show him that honesty is necessary in this world?" Teach yourself to think in the concrete instead of the abstract.

One of the stimulating things about this type of teaching is the fact that it becomes more interesting. Children learn facts more readily and the lessons become lasting impressions.

INVOLVED AND INTERESTED

Think of the different ways you might involve your pupils. Children learn best by doing!

"I was in a motion picture that our church made," Grace proudly and happily bragged.

"What did you do?" her friend asked.

"Oh, I carried the spear," she explained with a laugh, meaning that she was in a mob scene. But even though her part was small, she was happy about it. She felt the importance of the church's program because she had a part in it.

The Sunday school superintendent of that church appreciated the value of the well-known rule: "Children learn by doing." They also learn in other ways but usually they learn best by doing. When they once take an active part in a project they seldom forget it.

You and I can both look back at the times we became involved in activities at home, church, school, or in the community. We learned because action was involved on our part. Such experiences remain "big" in our minds. And through the years, those events mean much to us.

If you teach a Sunday school or home Bible class, think of the different ways you might involve your pupils. What can they do? How can they contribute to the lesson? Perhaps they can be drawn into a discussion.

How about having them sing? For instance, when you teach about the Lord Jesus stilling the waves, let the class sing softly an appropriate song.

Can they share some of their significant experiences? How did they earn the money to give to a missionary project?

Can they bring objects from home? Dolls in foreign dress? Stamps? Coins? Flowers for the worship center? An old family Bible? A scrapbook of newspaper clippings about Israel, Easter or Christmas?

Can you teach with sound effects? What about having the primary children march around the room to show how the children of Israel marched around the walls of Jericho?

There are so many things that youngsters can do. Some of them can read Bible passages. They can "act out" various character parts. They can say Bible verses in unison. They can trace, paint, color, cut out and paste. They can build. They can have class responsibilities. And surely they can raise questions!

If you are teaching a class, and using an object lesson, let one of the children hold the object. Permit the children to put up the flannelgraph and take down the figures. Let them distribute the song books and give out the memory verses. Some teachers let early-arriving children set the room in order, giving them a feeling that they are responsible for the class.

You, as a parent, can help your child sense the "spirit of Christmas" by letting him help in selecting the presents, in making the cookies, in wrapping gifts and taking them to the homes, especially of the confined or aging. Bess used to do these things with her mother. Now that she is older, she recalls them as her fondest Christmas memories. She did something for others and that made Christmas more meaningful.

Someone has cleverly characterized a child as "an active noise with some dirt on it." At least part of this is true: active! Loving parents and teachers will capitalize on this natural endowment. And by so doing, will use one of the best methods of teaching—*learning by doing*!

REMOTE OR RELATED

"Last night I received a phone call from an old time friend. He said . . ."

Just let the minister tell about some personal experience and instantly the "pew-sitters" become alert. They are interested when he mentions things they have done, places they have been, or thoughts they have had.

Teaching should be related to the child's interest and experience.

Successful speakers, writers and teachers constantly strive to do just this. Psychologists call it "identifying" with the listener. This technique of "tying-in" with the listeners is one of the best means you as a parent or teacher can use. You are *bound* to get through to youngsters if you relate to their own personal experiences. And it's easy to do!

Just remember this—when you explain or tell something to children, begin with an experience with which they are familiar.

Here's an example of the personalized approach when you are telling the Bible story of the boy with the five loaves and two fishes. Instead of beginning: "Our lesson today is about Jesus feeding the multitude," ask the class, "Have you ever been on a picnic? (pause) Of course you have!" And say, "Aren't they fun? When you go on a picnic there's one thing you always have plenty of. Yes, it's lots of good food! Now suppose you were on a picnic with enough food for yourself, but many, many people came and they were all very hungry. They didn't have a bite to eat and there was no place nearby where they could get any food. Wouldn't that be terrible? Now I know that you would be willing to share your lunch, but that wouldn't help because you wouldn't have enough for more than one or two. What do you think you would do? Well, I am going to tell you what one little boy did when this happened to him. This is a *real* story from the Bible, God's Word. Once there was a little boy who . . ."

When using this interesting approach, "tying-in" with their personal experiences, ask yourself these questions: (1) What do my children know? (2) How do they spend their time? and (3) What experiences have most of them had? Naturally, this means that you must be well acquainted with them. But this is part of being an effective teacher.

The reason that this method always meets with success is really quite subtle. A psychologist might come up with the following explanation: A child may not be aware of his feelings, and surely he cannot explain them. But unconsciously he *senses* that the teacher understands him, knows his interests, and has a feeling of concern in him as a personality.

So, as you look into the bright little eyes of children, ask yourself, "Is what I am saying to them *remote* or *related?*" Now you are taking steps to become a more effective parent or teacher!

EXTRANEOUS OR ESSENTIAL

"Where has the time gone?" This seems to be the common complaint of Sunday school teachers. We constantly face the concern of time slipping by without proper accomplishment.

One of the most serious handicaps a Sunday school teacher encounters is the extremely limited time that he has with his pupils. Parents are with their children for many years. Teachers in public and private schools are with their pupils for several hours a day. But, Sunday school teachers see their pupils for a brief period once every seven days. Consequently, these precious minutes must be used wisely.

Pupils should be protected from unnecessary interruptions.

Classes are often interrupted with roll calls, offerings, a host of announcements, passers-by and late-comers. Little techniques, however, can be learned to help offset this situation. Often the roll can be taken quietly by one of the more capable pupils. Taking attendance can be used as a time to reply with a memory verse. Offering envelopes can be passed around while announcements are being made, and the money quietly counted and recorded by one pupil.

One interruption which needs constant watching, is that caused by people walking by. It is only natural for a child to turn around and look at the passer-by. If possible, arrange to have your class where few people will want to pass. If this is impossible, see if you can place a screen or curtain between your class and the distraction. If nothing more can be done, train yourself to disregard those who walk by your teaching area. An irritated teacher is not a good Christian example. Make your lesson so appealing that your pupils are engrossed in what they are learning, rather than in the extraneous stimuli.

If your class is interrupted unduly you should speak to the head of your department or to the Sunday school superintendent himself. He may come up with a solution. If not, he can keep you in mind when other classrooms become available.

Whether at home or at school, the adult should help children to learn by protecting them from nonessential interruptions. Occasional distractions may be annoying, but constant ones can be fatal. In the Sunday school continual distractions rob children of spiritual food which builds character and feeds their souls. In life, they rob a person of purpose and precious time!

COMPLIMENT OR CRITICISM

I was seventeen and a freshman in college. It was my first weekend at home. Thanksgiving time was near and

I had a wonderful, exciting feeling as I dashed up the broad cement steps to the old general store in our ranching community. Mr. Walton, a stately old gentleman, and a leader in the community, came out of the store just as I reached the top of the steps. "Well, look at you," he said, as he shook my hand. "It's good to see you, son. How are you making out at college?"

"Oh, pretty well, I guess."

Encouragement is a necessary part of every successful parent's and teacher's equipment.

"Well, let me tell you something, my boy," he continued. "Everybody in the community is looking to you.

33

We're all as proud of you as can be, and we know you're going to break all the records at that school."

I didn't remember anything else that happened on that weekend. I seemed to be up on "cloud number seven" for the rest of the year. In fact, it gave me a thrill every time I thought about what my friend had said. And I suppose ten years passed by before it ever occurred to me that what he said might not have been completely factual!

That's the way encouragement works. It gives you a lift and makes you do "more than you're capable of doing." Research studies show that children who are praised and encouraged accomplish more than those who are shamed and criticized. Success one time predisposes a person to success the next.

Encouragement is part of every successful parent's and teacher's equipment. Children are not so interested in "great achievement" as they are in daily progress. You may not be able to praise a child for advancing a mile, but you *can* give him recognition for moving ahead an inch.

Children sometimes feel that they aren't successful unless they are told so. As a parent or teacher, you are responsible for encouraging your children. As a Christian, you have even more responsibility because you are feeding not only their minds, but their souls.

Scolding only arouses antagonism in a child or adult. They sulk, taking the attitude, "Well if I'm no good, I won't try." Even correction should be based on the admittance that a child is able to do better.

An outstanding teacher told me once, "I try to compliment or encourage every child in my class, individually, each Sunday. I find it does something for them and it does a *lot* for me."

If you are not accustomed to encouraging each of your children regularly, try it and you will see how really important it is. Individual recognition costs so little, yet the benefits are many!

SELF OR SPIRIT

Miss Larson was a smartly-dressed, well-educated Sunday school teacher, but she was not especially effective in the classroom. One day, when talking to the Sunday school superintendent, she said, "I don't know what's the matter with those kids. I don't get any place with them. I think someone else could do a much better job with them than I."

The superintendent knew Miss Larson's ability. He talked to her sympathetically. After several conferences he

"All things through Christ which strengtheneth me."

was able to give her much spiritual help. She came to realize that she was teaching in her own strength, that her lack of devotion to the Lord prevented her from being used effectively to reach boys and girls. She wasn't spending enough time alone with the Lord in prayer, and reading His Word. Although a Christian, worldly things held her interest. Christ was not preeminent in her life.

After much prayer, the teacher did give full control of her life to the Lord. Then her heart was filled with love and God blessed her ministry of teaching. Several children gave their lives to Christ. Others were noticeably drawn closer to Him. Teaching became a joy.

She was a living example of the truth that "man's ways are not God's ways," as the Scripture says, "For my thoughts are not your thoughts, neither are your ways my ways, saith the LORD" (Isaiah 55:8).

As Christians, our efforts are in vain unless they are energized by the Holy Spirit. God makes this plain when He says, "I am the vine, ye are the branches: He that abideth in me, and I in him, the same bringeth forth much fruit: for without me ye can do nothing" (John 15:5).

This truth has great significance to parents as well as to teachers. God wants us to be well-trained, but first of all, He wants us to be men and women who are wholly dedicated to Him. If there has to be a choice, deep spirituality is much preferred to "technical know-how." As a psychologist, I am keenly aware of the importance of excellent training. But as I work with parents and teachers, I am deeply convinced that their greatest single need is close fellowship with the Lord Jesus Christ!

If you have not been effective in teaching or training your children, it may be due to spiritual immaturity. Actually, as a parent or teacher, you are in partnership with God. He is the One who empowers. In a real sense you are like a wire that conducts electricity from its source to an object. And the place of connection is the quiet time spent with Him.

The training of your child, or the boys and girls you teach, is too vital to let anything divert or hinder the working of the Holy Spirit. The consequences reach all through this life and on into eternal life! God wants these lives for Himself. You need His help to bring them to Him! Efforts expended in your own strength will avail but little. As expressed by the poet, Lucy Alice Perkins:

> Oh, partnership divine,
>   That Thou dost work with me!
> What wealth and power are mine,
>   Since I may work with Thee!

CHAPTER TWO

Ages and Stages

If you wish to study men, you must not neglect to mix with the society of children.—*Jesse Torrey*

GROWING

ONE OF THE greatest joys in life is observing children as they enter various stages of development. Although all children pass through similar developmental sequences, they may not necessarily do so at the same age.

To work most effectively with a child, one must understand his individual pattern and rate of growth. For every child there is no doubt a period in his development when he can best succeed at any given activity. In other words, children are physically, mentally and emotionally ready for certain tasks at certain times.

Wise teachers and parents take many of their cues from the developmental sequences through which their children are passing. To challenge a child at a time when he is approaching sufficient maturity to accomplish an activity of his own interest, may well mean the difference between success and failure in that activity.

Children may be expected to differ widely from others their own age. There is no "typical" five, six, seven, or eight-year-old, because each one is different. There are, however, general characteristics and needs which apply to many children at certain age levels. The developmental characteristics outlined in this section are intended (a) to give teachers and parents a concise guide for understanding boys and girls, and (b) to indicate effective ways of working with children.

PHYSICAL DEVELOPMENT

Specialists in child growth and development tell us that if we continued to grow at the same rate *after* we were born, as we did *before* we were born, by the time we reached the age of twenty, each of us would be several times larger than the moon! So once again we see God's marvelous master plan in the physical development of the human body. From the time a child is born until he reaches adolescence, his rate of growth gradually slows down.

If you work with five, six, seven and eight-year-olds, you will notice this "slowing down" growth process. An interesting observation is the fact that girls are usually ahead of boys in general maturity. We know that most girls at about twelve years of age are as much as two years ahead of boys the same age in their maturity. This difference in development begins to manifest itself years before they enter adolescence. In fact, it is noticeable even in the kindergarten. This is normal and natural. God made them that way.

Primary age children are very "wiggly" little people. They are not adept at sitting still for long periods of time. Often we see them doing tricks, turning somersaults, or hanging by their knees. Restlessness and nervousness may be indications that teachers and parents are not providing enough activity for them. The wise teacher will plan a program which offers opportunity for plenty of physical activity. Sprinkle motion songs and marching activities in between "listening" periods. Otherwise, you may not hold their interest. Children learn best through active participation, and children between the ages of five and eight enjoy involving their entire bodies in whatever they do.

Although the young child's coordination is steadily improving he does not yet have full control of small muscles.

This is the reason some children find it difficult to write or cut well. To do handwork that requires much skill or control is a real effort for them. However, there is no cause for concern because this needed coordination will develop as time goes on.

By the time a child is five years old, he usually speaks quite clearly. If he does not develop clear speech during kindergarten, seriously consider contacting your school psychologist, a pediatrician, or speech therapist. Through proper attention your child may be spared years of embarrassment by having to be the victim of a speech handicap.

Most children are definitely left-handed or right-handed by the time they are five. Be sensitive to your child's handedness. Let him develop naturally. Forcing a left-handed child to become right-handed (and vice versa) may result in emotional conflicts, speech difficulties and other problems.

Most children of this age are far-sighted, thus requiring large objects for work and play. Eye strain may be evidenced at about seven years of age. Parents and teachers should not over-emphasize activities which require too much close eye work. By eight, the child's eyes are beginning to accommodate more readily to both near and far distances. Near sightedness usually develops during this year.

Primary children require alternate periods of rest and activity with plenty of sleep each night. They will also benefit from your guidance in nutritional care. Make sure their meals come at regular times, and that they eat at least a few bites of various foods on the table. When mealtime is made a happy time and they are taught the value of food, most of your "feeding" problems will disappear.

INTELLECTUAL DEVELOPMENT

I shall never forget the time my little daughter climbed up on my lap, and with sparkling eyes said, "Daddy, teach me something." As I gave her a real tight hug and a kiss I thought to myself, *That's the way all children are. They want to learn.*

Children enjoy learning because their intellects are developing. With each day of development comes the ability to understand a little more. Like climbing up a mountain, each step lifts you a bit higher so that you can see a little farther, and gain a better perspective.

Primary children are not only inquisitive, but variable. They change their minds frequently and go from one activity to another. Parents and teachers should not expect them to give their full attention to the subject for more than just a few minutes. A change of activities will help the child tremendously. And, of course, the younger the child, the shorter his attention span.

An important thing to keep in mind about five-year-olds is that although they are able to start to school—entering the wonderful new experience of kindergarten—they are not sufficiently mature to do "school work." The "three R's" should wait until children are about six or six and one-half years old. There is no virtue in pushing him ahead of his God-given readiness. In fact, physical and emotional damage can be done when over-anxious adults place demands upon children before they are ready to assume them.

Primary children, especially seven and eight-year-olds, are usually interested in anything that runs on wheels. They prefer skates to tricycles, and are anxious to have "bikes." They like cars, trains, airplanes—and want to know how they work. They enjoy painting, moulding clay, and using simple carpentry tools. Filling their pockets with an assortment of collections is also part of being a seven or eight-year-old.

Eight-year-olds are eager to try all sorts of things. They like softball and other organized games. They thrill to stories about adventure. They enjoy crafts, and often demonstrate considerable skill in handling tools. They run, shout, climb, wrestle, and punch. They can't always carry through their games by themselves, but they do respond to adults who are friendly and helpful. An occasional afternoon outing for a third grade group will often prove more effective than a thousand words in a Sunday school class.

As a consulting psychologist in a large school system, I find that during the primary years many slow developing children are identified for the first time. After a year or so of school experience most classroom teachers can easily spot the boys and girls who are slow in their maturation. Comparisons with other children make intellectual and other differences quite evident. Parents should talk with the teacher in order to learn about the child's development. If a child is apparently much slower than other children, he should be referred to the school psychologist or guidance director. After testing the child and observing him on the playground and in the classroom the psychologist can give parents professional counsel. Wise parents will accept such findings, then cooperate with school authorities in setting up a program to help the child.

The average I. Q. is 100. In other words, children of average intelligence show a 100 per cent correlation between their physical age and their mental age. For example, the average child who is just seven years of age is also seven years old mentally. He thinks, grasps ideas, and "catches on" like most seven-year-olds. A child who has an intelligence quotient of 120 is considerably brighter than most children his age. On the other hand, a child who has an intelligence quotient of 80 is less intelligent than the average child his age.

A considerable amount of importance is placed on intelligence because it indicates a child's potential ability to learn. It may also give clues concerning the causes of his behavior.

Strange as it may seem, the average child is average. Stranger yet is the fact that no child is average! "Wait a minute," you say. "Let's say that again!"

Here's the explanation: Most of the children with whom we work are not especially bright or especially dull. They are just average—about like other children. This calls for a simple, clear, attractive approach.

On the other hand, children who make an average score on intelligence tests usually have some abilities slightly above the average point, and some abilities slightly below. When these "above" and "below" abilities are added, the result is "average." That is why most "average" children work both above and below their age level.

There are, of course, some children who are much more, or much less intelligent than others their age. If these children are enjoying good physical and mental health, their superior or inferior ability might be attributed to natural differences. This is usually determined at the time of conception—nine months before they are born. Hence, nagging at a child or pressuring him doesn't change his natural endowment. It only places an additional burden on him—an emotional one. Wise indeed is the parent or teacher who carefully challenges each youngster to do his best without putting undue pressure on him. These intellectual differences have many important implications. Basically, you will be wise to ask yourself these questions: "By giving the entire class the same thing to do, what handicaps am I placing on some of the children?" "What advantages am I giving others?"

EMOTIONAL DEVELOPMENT

It was Monday night, and the members of the church building committee were meeting in the pastor's office. "Well, men," asked the chairman, "are we about ready to take a vote?"

"You can count me out," retorted Steve Davis. "You fellows don't need me on this committee. My ideas don't count very much around here. I've gotta go anyway. Maybe you can get someone else who'll go along with you."

The men were left "cold" as Steve stormed out of the room. *He's like a two-year-old,* they thought. *He's never grown up.*

And so there are many adults much like Steve. They've never grown up—emotionally immature. In fact, one of the biggest jobs that faces parents and teachers is that of helping children to develop emotionally.

It is difficult indeed to indicate the emotional development of children at various age levels. Perhaps it is more important to know the emotional *needs* of boys and girls.

Psychologists and psychiatrists are in general agreement that there are several basic psychological and emotional needs. These must be met if children are to grow up to be mature men and women.

The following is an outline of these needs. By keeping them in mind, you can help children to develop normally and eventually function as mature, effective adults.

1. During the early years, a child should have the assurance that he belongs—that he is desired, and that in his absence he is missed. To him constant criticism means that he doesn't suit, that he is not wanted and that he does not belong.

2. Children need to feel that they are achieving and being successful. Their tasks should be appropriate to their own ability. Material rewards are not as satisfying as personal compliments and encouragement.

3. The life of a small boy or girl should be relatively free from fear. Merely telling a child not to be afraid, doesn't remove the fear. Sympathetic discussion and reasoning is always helpful.

When a child shows embarrassment, and it is damaging to him, the adult can step in and give him support. Discipline should not be gained by frequent use of threats.

4. Children of all ages need much love and affection. They not only need to be loved; they need to be told that they are loved. Our love should not be provisional. We should never tell them that we, or that God loves them only when they are good.

5. Feelings of guilt and blame should be minimized. Children like adults, are not perfect, and it does a child little good to be constantly blamed. Simply accusing a child does not offer a solution. He should not be led to believe that anyone other than God is perfect. Past unpleasant behavior should be minimized. Children should be taught to pray and to ask God's forgiveness of sin.

6. Naturally, young children cannot contribute to the

family as much as older ones. But they need the feeling of contributing, just as though they were older. We should think of ways to include small children so that they know they have a share in the activities of the home and Sunday school. We cannot afford to overlook a child's contribution, no matter how small it is.

7. It is natural for children to inquire and to desire knowledge. Their questions are important to them, even though they may not always interest adults. We should take children's questions seriously. Probably more important than the answer we give, is the cordial, happy manner in which we receive their questions.

8. Another need of all children is that of feeling economically secure. This security is not dependent upon financial resources. Rather, it is dependent upon emphasis given to material things. All parents and teachers can help children feel that they have the important things in life, and that God will provide all their needs as they trust Him.

9. No doubt, the greatest need of children is to have an abiding faith in God. Human beings are spiritual beings and as such their personalities are never fully developed unless they have many experiences which develop their faith. Parents and teachers can make a unique contribution by teaching little ones about God who created them, and who is personally interested in them.

Adults should be sensitive to a child's understanding, and at an appropriate time encourage him to accept Christ as his personal Savior.

SOCIAL DEVELOPMENT

Boys and girls between the ages of five and eight are interested in other children, but they are more interested in themselves. They want the group to like and accept them, yet they sometimes find it difficult to play together. This is especially true of five and six-year-old who usually get along best with just one or two.

In group games boys and girls enjoy playing together, but their interests are beginning to diverge. This is especially noticeable at about the seven-year-old level. By the second and third grade, their best friends are nearly always of the same sex. By this time they have become "curiously exclusive." If parents and teachers could only remember how they felt about the opposite sex when they were eight, they would not tease children or cause them needless embarrassment.

By the time a child is seven, he can express himself remarkably well. It is not unusual for him to use this ability against others. Instead of fighting he may prefer to throw words at a playmate, then leave the scene. The playground is usually getting a little rougher and this is one of his ways of "holding his own."

Youngsters at seven and eight want a "best friend." This may mean arguments and quarrels. But they should usually be permitted to work out these situations without too much adult interference.

Besides his playmates and his family, the primary child is sometimes confronted with another adjustment upon the arrival of a new baby brother or sister. This usually means that he has to leave the throne so that another younger and "cuter" one can be crowned king. This is not an easy thing for a young child to take. Parents should talk about the new baby which is to come into their home. Explaining what the wee one will be like and how he will need constant care is a very important preparation for the acceptance of the "new-comer." Make the child feel that the baby belongs to him as well as to Mother and Daddy. With a reasonable amount of explanation and special attention your child will eventually learn to be happy about a new member of the family.

These adjustments to other people are *learned*. And adults have the joy of teaching them. The responsibility parents and teachers have for helping children make good social adjustments is especially significant. Nearly everything in the child's future is affected by his skill in accepting and working with other people. It *is* important!

EDUCATIONAL DEVELOPMENT

The first few years of school are important ones. At this time the child is leaving home to associate (and usually compete) with other children. This calls for many new adjustments. He feels strange and insecure. Now is a crucial time in his development when he needs parents and teachers who are sympathetic and understanding. The feelings you give him at this age are likely to last for many years. He may forget much of what he is taught, but he is not likely to forget the personalities who taught him, the sort of persons his parents and teachers were, and how they made him feel.

Although most children are ready for simple word and number concepts at about six and one-half years of age, some are not ready until later. Wise adults are sensitive to the child's readiness for new tasks. Interest is an indication of readiness to learn. Too much emphasis on school achievement can destroy his confidence, create tension, and make learning much harder. Parents and teachers should cooperate with the maturity which they find in children at each age level. The primary classroom should be a place where children are challenged at their own level, rather than a place where all boys and girls are required to meet inflexible, predetermined standards.

The five-year-old is not ready for formal reading, writing and arithmetic. But he can learn many other important things such as getting along with others, taking turns, following directions and gaining the necessary skills for learning readiness. His progress in the first grade the following year, will depend largely upon his background as a five-year-old.

If parents and teachers try to force too much formal study on the five and six-year-old—before he is ready for it, he will react in various ways. He may become quite aggressive, hitting back at the people who expect too much of him. On the other hand he may sense that he is not equal to the situation, and withdraw most of the time. He will grow to dislike the situation where he is placed under pressure and will resent all that goes with it. His reactions will not be desirable ones and they will probably leave lasting impressions.

Primary boys and girls should not be exploited for the sake of a finished product or for perfection. Expect mistakes and much forgetting. Remember, they are only beginners in this "big business" of learning.

Teach him about his immediate environment—his home, community, Sunday school. You can help by talking with him about the things he sees and hears. By the time children are eight, they usually understand about days, months and years. However, discussions of events that occurred centuries ago, may be confusing to them. Their concept of time is not fully developed.

In the primary grades "story time" is very important. Your child will learn *so* much from stories you read to him, especially if you discuss them. But just as important as the knowledge he acquires is the sweet love he feels as he sits with his parents or teacher enjoying these stories!

If homework in the second or third grade is indicated, make it a happy experience. If it is an unpleasant time, it probably will do as much harm as it does good.

It is not unusual for girls in the first, second and third grades to achieve good grades more easily than boys. This is especially true in the language arts—reading, spelling and communication. This is due to: (1) a natural, advanced maturity and (2) home activities that give young girls more experience in such things. Knowing this, you will avoid putting pressure on boys in the primary grades. Give them time and they will naturally overcome this disadvantage at school.

BEHAVIOR DEVELOPMENT

"My, my, my," bubbled Aunt Susan as she greeted Mrs. Brown and her six-year-old son. Then turning to the boy, Aunt Susan spoke the words that have been repeated a million times, "Your baby is growing up!"

Of course children do grow up, but they also grow *away*. The older a child becomes the more he wants to grow away from his parents and family and to learn about the larger world about him. When you have cared for a child from infancy, it may be difficult to realize that he has grown so much and that by now he is ready to do a lot on his own. Naturally, the tendency is to do for him what he can do for himself because he takes so long and doesn't do it well. Yet it is most important that children be permitted to do things by themselves for this is the way they learn to become self-confident and successful.

Once I had a conference with a mother who was seriously concerned about her child. It was evident to me that she was not willing to let him grow up. Without realizing it, she tried to dominate his every move. For example, although he was old enough, she never permitted the child to put tooth paste on his own tooth brush. "Oh, Dr. Narramore," she exclaimed, "I wouldn't think of letting him do that. I'm afraid he'd squirt it all over the walls and floor."

I thought to myself, "What is a parent for? Naturally she'd have to guide him several times until he did it acceptably, but within a few days she would have him on his own."

Welcome the young child's bid for independence. Help him help himself. You can do this by reasoning with him about what he should do, and encouraging him to make many choices for himself. Your child needs a helping hand but be sure you don't direct his activities too closely.

In the Scriptures we read, "A merry heart doeth good like a medicine . . ." (Prov. 17:22). This certainly applies to child psychology. You'll enjoy children much more (and help them too) if you maintain a sense of humor as you work with them. Children aren't little adults. There's no rhyme or reason to some of the things they do. Just chalk it up to "childhood" and laugh about it! This ability to smile with youngsters will develop your own patience. The results will be big in dividends.

Is dawdling a problem? Why not try "racing!" It works. Threats won't speed him very much. Such ultimatums aren't too good for either of you. As far as you are concerned, they usually just result in another ulcer.

Seven and eight-year-olds characteristically have more enthusiasm than they do wisdom. But they do not want to be treated like younger children. They like responsibility because they want to be recognized by adults and do the things that they consider grown-up. Don't talk down to them. They'll be sure to sense the fact that you are not recognizing their "maturity."

Second and third graders have considerable ability to evaluate themselves. They are capable of developing a fairly accurate mental check list of what they have done that's good, and what is poor. Encourage them to talk about their own behavior. This is time well spent in any home or Sunday school class. They have a strong sense of justice. They want "rights" to win, and "wrongs" to lose, to be blamed or punished. So expect much arguing—and remember, five to eight-year groups need supervision.

At eight, children are completing their primary years and getting ready to enter the more mature middle years. Differences in them are especially noticeable at this time. Allow for different rates in growth—both physical and mental. They may not be as easy to guide as they were a year earlier, but that is part of growing up.

Children who are taught to obey parents and teachers are at a great advantage. They find it easier to adjust to life, and make friends. Adults should expect reasonable obedience, yet keep discipline threats and ultimatums at a minimum.

You might keep this in mind: All behavior is caused. There are reasons why your child acts as he does. Look for causes for unacceptable behavior. Be alert to possible causes before you decide what steps to take. Perhaps the first thing to do is to look at yourself! Are you tired, irritable, "on edge?" Such emotional strains are "catching." You'll probably discover that nine times out of ten, if *you* are feeling happy and relaxed, there are very few problems with your child. However, when punishment is necessary, quietly explain the reason for it. This makes it more justifiable to the child and it has a tendency to prevent him from deliberately doing the wrong thing again.

Your aim in discipline should be this: *self discipline*. It you work well with your child, as he grows older he will learn to control himself without the constant aid of adults. This requires wisdom and patience on your part. As you discipline your child keep asking yourself, "Is this helping him establish standards of acceptable conduct? Does this encourage and show him how to control himself?"

TIPS ON BEHAVIOR

1. Avoid unnecessary clashes of will. Why make an issue of it? It's possible, you know, to argue about *everything*. This doesn't mean that you should always give in. Not at all. But it does imply some give and take.

2. Keep rigid standards at a minimum. Human beings just aren't machines. Standards are all right but rigid ones are seldom helpful. Life is a series of adjustments.

3. Show children how to be thoughtful of others; to take turns. Thoughtfulness does not come naturally. It must be learned. Furthermore, instruction about thoughtfulness is an on-going process; it requires review. Naturally your own example is more effective than many words.

4. Give children responsibilites in the home and in the classroom. But avoid undue pressure. Some of the obvious signs of excessive pressure are fatigue, crying, nervous habits, day dreaming, forgetfulness and confusion.

5. Beware of too much criticism. It seldom offers a solution, and it tends to sever ties of friendliness and confidence.

6. Distract a child from undesirable behavior. Call his attention to a different activity. This is easily done and it usually avoids a clash.

7. Patiently teach your child what is, and what is not his. Explain why. Back up your explanation by giving him a place for his own belongings. And see to it that *his* property rights (as well as yours) are respected.

8. Encourage a child to tell how he feels about things. Talk to him in a quiet, calm manner. The result? It helps

him to clarify his own thinking, and it gives you understanding as to why he acts the way he does.

9. Give the child some part in family planning. Discuss things as a group. Offer several acceptable choices. A young child's part in planning may be small to you, but big and important to him.

10. Prepare children for the day's activities by discussing with them what is to take place, and approximately how long it will require. Get them emotionally "ready" to go and to do. This predisposes them to do it and to do so happily.

11. Assure children of God's love, regardless of their behavior. Never give them the impression that God doesn't care for them, even though God does not accept their behavior.

12. Pray with a child individually about his problems, fears and uncertainties. Then, parent or teacher, *you* go alone and pray *for* him. This will change "Johnny" and it may change you!

CHAPTER THREE

Spiritual Development

And these words, which I command thee this day, shall be in thine heart: And thou shalt teach them diligently unto thy children, and shalt talk of them when thou sittest in thine house, and when thou walkest by the way, and when thou liest down, and when thou risest up.

—*The Bible* (Deut. 6:6, 7)

YOU CAN WIN YOUR CHILD

"PERHAPS PARENTS and teachers would work with new zeal and vision if they stopped to realize that the film of childhood can never be run through for a second showing." This is how Evelyn Nown, children's specialist, has expressed this urgent truth. The statement brings us all face to face with the brevity and importance of childhood. It is a vital time. You hear it on all sides, but have you considered the extreme urgency of working with children? If you don't reach them *today* you may not be able to reach them *tomorrow.*

Childhood days are the most impressionable ones. Although research studies show that children are especially impressionable during their early years, I never cease to marvel at this startling fact when I am called upon to give psychological examinations. Life patterns *do* emerge remarkably early.

The shaping of those patterns is the parents' responsibility. We parents are in somewhat the same situation as the woman who dreamed that a little elf was sitting at the foot of her bed, holding her son by the hand. Frightened, she asked, "What are you going to do with him?"

"I don't know," replied the elf. "It's your dream."

Yes, it is up to us. A child is not an organism left to wander aimlessly until he assumes some kind of philosophy of life. Each one has a soul that will live somewhere forever. God tells us that "Children are an heritage of the LORD" (Ps. 127:3). They are God's gift to us, to be trained for His glory. In His matchless Word, He tells us, "And all thy children shall be taught of the LORD: and great shall be the peace of the children" (Isa. 54:13).

To take raw material of childhood and to mold it into godly adulthood is a job requiring the cooperation of both parents. Unfortunately, there is not always Christian teamwork between parents. Sometimes one parent alone is interested in the spiritual welfare of the children. In this situation the spiritually concerned parent runs into real difficulty in raising the children for Christ. Yet, he can essentially overcome the handicap if he is patient and if he relies upon the Lord. The parent may not be able to reach his children in some ways, but he can reach them in others. This section of *How to Understand and Influence Children* is devoted to different ways you can win your child to the Lord.

Your greatest job as a parent is winning them, for as the poet says, these are "The Plastic Years."

> They pass so quickly, the days of youth
> And the children change so fast,
> And soon they harden in the mould,
> And the plastic years are past.
>
> Then shape their lives while they are young,
> This be our prayer, our aim,
> That every child we meet, shall bear
> The imprint of His name.
> —*Author Unknown*

FAMILY DEVOTIONS

There were three Nelson boys, tall, sturdy and blonde. Time passed, and when they reached adulthood they became outstanding, godly men. The parents were grateful and daily thanked God for His guiding hand in the lives of their sons. But the spiritual success of these men was a natural outgrowth of their childhood homelife. The boys had been trained in the Lord, and the heart of the training was the family's daily devotional time.

Among all Christian activities, few, if any, are more important than daily family devotions. Attendance at church and prayer meeting, as important as they are, can never take the place of the family altar. Here is where you develop Christian character, receive godly instruction, and learn to walk intimately with the Lord. God emphasizes the importance of daily instruction in the home when He says, "And these words, which I command thee this day, shall be in thine heart: and thou shalt teach them diligently unto thy children, and shalt talk of them when thou sittest in thine house, and when thou walkest by the way, and when thou liest down, and when thou risest up" (Deut. 6:6,7).

One can imagine that as God looks upon us each day, nothing rejoices His heart more than seeing a family gathered around the Bible, worshiping, praying and learning of Him. Even a very short time of devotions is valuable. Spiritual food is like other food. It should be eaten daily if it is to do the most good.

"But," you ask, "what should a parent do if his mate refuses to cooperate in having family devotions?" Of course this conditions poses a hardship. However, you can make the best of it. Daily devotions with your children are so important that they must not be abandoned. If it is impossible to have group devotions, have *individual* ones. If you can't arrange for a most desirable amount of time, use a shorter period. You may have to adapt a more flexible schedule in order to find a suitable time. Also, do not schedule family devotions in a way or at a time that they would needlessly antagonize your mate. If you earnestly seek God's guidance, He will make it possible for you to continue this important method of influencing your children for Christ.

Family devotions should begin with "a joyful noise unto God" (Ps. 66:1). Singing praises unto the Lord refreshes the soul. During the day we may forget some of the Bible reading or our memory verses, but the melody of the song will often linger in our heart.

Naturally, reading the Bible is a very important part of the period. This is God speaking to you. There are many different methods of Bible reading. You can follow the selected passages of a devotional guide. You can follow the passages suggested for your Sunday school lesson, or you can read the Bible through from beginning to end, repeating the process until the family is well acquainted with the entire book. When so doing, there will be some parts which you will want to skip with very young children, such as the "begats," the detailed description of the tabernacle, and some of the strictly historical passages. However, we know that "All scripture is given by inspiration of God, and is profitable for doctrine, for reproof, for correction, for instruction in righteousness" (II Tim 3:16).

In addition to the Bible, a number of excellent supplementary materials are available, such as Bible story and devotional books.

After your period of Bible and devotional reading there could well be a time for Scripture memorization.

This should be followed by the important time of prayer. It is encouraging to have a definite prayer list to which you can refer each day. It will strengthen your faith to check off requests as they are answered, remembering that the Lord answers "yes"—"no"—and sometimes "later."

After such experiences, it is almost impossible to persuade a child that God does not answer prayer. He *knows* God does, and he has written down and crossed off prayer requests himself.

Prayer should be such a normal part of your family life that it will automatically be the same for your child. As he grows up he will realize that it isn't something accidentally attached to life. Rather, it is vital contact with Almighty God, an intimate talk with a good friend.

Prayers need not be long. Instead, short prayers should be encouraged so as not to discourage the younger children. But, when being short, beware of being repetitious. There is a sterility in dusty, routine words, and unfortunately, too many are used when we talk to God. Be fresh in your thinking, otherwise your children will regard prayer as oral arithmetic ... a mere adding of words. For instance, instead of simply saying, "Bless Mary" try to think of what blessing would be especially beneficial to Mary. God has many choice blessings if you ask for them.

Let your devotional time be one of sweet fellowship with God and each other. Wrongs can be righted, praise can be offered for blessings and answered prayer, and serenity can be displayed in the midst of trouble.

These are times of unprecedented evil and confusion. Our courts are overcrowded with juvenile criminals and delinquents. Our mental institutions are unable to admit thousands who cannot maintain a dynamic balance amid the stresses and strains of life. In view of our troubled times, Christian families cannot afford to neglect daily devotions. They keep us spiritually strong. They are the primary source from which our children learn to pray and understand God's Word. They form a bond of fellowship about the family circle that is even sweeter and stronger than its human ties. Family devotions fortify us against the temptations and emergencies of life. To the Christian family there is nothing that pays greater dividends. There is no greater challenge!

SCRIPTURE MEMORIZATION

Ralph had not attended church for years. One day he surprised his wife, Gwen, when he said, "Honey, how about my going to church with you this Sunday?"

"What?" exclaimed Gwen, noticeably surprised.

"I just said," repeated Ralph, "How about my going to church with you Sunday?"

"Well, of course. Sure! I'd love it! You know that, darling, but I, well, I was just a little surprised that you wanted to go."

And on Sunday they *did* go to church. As time went on, Ralph attended regularly, and eventually he took his stand for the Lord. Finally Ralph told his wife what brought him back to God.

"It was those Bible verses," he said. "I learned a lot of them when I was a kid, and they never left me. I couldn't get them out of my mind. They kept coming back. Finally I just gave up and went back to church."

As with Ralph, so with many others. God's word is powerful and it does not return unto Him void. Rest assured that as you help a child memorize Scripture, you are giving him the most important thing in the world.

The greatest knowledge one can have is an understanding of the Word of God. By it we have eternal life through Christ. It is a flawless guide for living! Knowledge of Scripture combats wrong teachings and unsound doctrines. It prevents children from becoming entangled in "isms" and cults, and it will keep them from sin. "Thy word have I hid in mine heart that I might not sin against thee" (Ps. 119:11).

So, it is most important that you as a parent or teacher help your children memorize Bible verses. They will enjoy hiding the Word of God in their hearts.

Here are some tips on memorization:

1. *Give each verse a "title."* It will help your children understand the verse and it aids in recalling it when needed. Example: Ephesians 2:8 might be titled, "Saved Through Faith."

2. *Write the verses.* Put the verses and their references on handy 2 x 3½ cards. You can buy these white linen cards at most variety stores. They can be conveniently carried and referred to during the day. Or, at religious bookstores you can buy packs of cards with the verses printed on them. Also, The Navigators, Colorado Springs, Colorado, have an excellent memory course, with which they furnish packs of small cards in a holder. The price is three dollars.

3. *Read verses alternately.* It helps to memorize the verses if one individual reads the verse, then another member. Additional voices and emphasis impress different parts of the verse upon the mind. After several have read the same verse, one person can say the first part, followed by another saying the remaining parts of it. Then switch parts. Then all say it together—then individually. It's fun, yet effective.

4. *Discuss the verse.* This gives it added meaning. Discussion helps to "tie it" closely to one's life. Understanding should always come before drill. It is helpful to learn a verse, then use it through the week in actual situations. Compare experiences with each other. For instance, you might use, "And call upon me in the day of trouble: I will deliver thee, and thou shalt glorify me" (Ps. 50:15).

5. *Review a little each day.* Retaining verses takes constant review. When a person learns one or more verses each week, he will need to review them regularly. Also it is helpful to set up a monthly review, going over all the verses memorized during that period.

6. *Start memorization young.* Even three and four-year-

olds can learn portions of verses. But don't encourage them to "parrot." It will be meaningless to them. Rather, pick a phrase or two, such as, "Be ye kind" (Eph. 4:32), or "God is love" (I John 4:8). As they grow older they can learn entire verses. But when they are so young, be sensitive to their abilities. Let them learn what they can, and don't sacrifice the joy of learning God's Word for perfection.

7. *Give the award of praise.* Although little gift rewards for Scripture memorization are appreciated by children, one of the best rewards is genuine, personal recognition. Tell a youngster that he is doing well. Have the rest of the family or Sunday school class listen attentively while he is reciting. Let him know what a success he is.

A BIBLE-BELIEVING CHURCH

Churches, churches everywhere—down the block, across the street, two blocks over, or next door. Each one claims to be the best church. Some people claim that all roads lead to heaven. Unfortunately they don't, any more than all roads lead to New York or Chicago. Some churches are right. Some are wrong. Being run by men, many of them are partly right and partly wrong, but some are definitely more right than others.

It is your privilege as well as your responsibility to take your children to a Bible-believing church. Never risk sending them to a church or Sunday school where the clear, simple plan of salvation is not presented. There may be temptations to compromise, but remember, your children's souls are at stake. We know there are churches that do not preach the Gospel. God has warned us that in the last days people will turn from Bible teaching to diluted, unsound doctrine. "For the time will come when they will not endure sound doctrine: but after their own lusts shall they heap to themselves teachers, having itching ears: and they shall turn away their ears from the truth, and shall be turned unto fables" ((II Tim. 4:3, 4).

Seriously consider the church that you and your children are attending. Listen carefully to what the minister says, and also note things which he omits. Make sure that your church:

1. Preaches the Bible, and does not present some other book as equal. For instance, the Christian Science Church puts *Science and Health* by Mary Baker Eddy side by side with the Bible.

2. Teaches the entire Bible and not just isolated verses. Many cults take a handful of Scripture out of the context to prove their points. This is highly deceptive. If you wonder about the minister, ask him if he believes the entire Bible to be the Word of God.

3. Believes in the deity and the virgin birth of the Lord Jesus Christ. It is not enough to believe that Jesus Christ was a good man who had the misfortune of being crucified, but that He is the very Son of God.

4. Shows people how to be saved, using such verses as, "That if thou shalt confess with thy mouth the Lord Jesus, and shalt believe in thine heart that God hath raised him from the dead, thou shalt be saved" (Rom. 10:8, 10).

What should you do when a Catholic or a spiritually uninterested mate tries to convince you that he is to have complete control of raising the children? Obey God. But do so in love. Giving your children over to the unsaved is certainly not Scriptural. Even though circumstances may not permit you to take your children to a Bible-centered church regularly, you *can* take them to one at least part of the time.

Many parents have had the experience of finding Christ, then realizing that their own church was not suitable because they and their children were not given spiritual food. They have had to visit other churches until they found one where they could grow spiritually. It is not always easy to break away from a familiar church, but you can't afford *not* to. In a Christ-centered church you will soon have many new friends. You can join whole-heartedly all church activities. And, of course, you will mature spiritually. Such a change will wonderfully affect your family for life.

SONGS

The keynote of all harmonies. He planned
God is its author, and not man. He laid
All perfect combinations, and He made
Us so that we could hear and understand.
                                    —*Author Unknown*

Music is a universal language—"the most perfect symbol of life."

Long before a child starts to investigate the fascinating world right outside his door, music wings its way to him and like a guileless extrovert, looks for signs of welcome. And the signs are there. The child gurgles and claps and moves to the rhythm of the music. From his response it is obvious that the child has found a new affection, one that will last a lifetime. It will be one that you can effectively use to influence your children for Christ.

Many Christians have said that next to the Bible, hymns carry the greatest gospel message. God's Word tells us, "Let the word of Christ dwell in you richly in all wisdom, teaching and admonishing one another in psalms and hymns and spiritual songs, singing with grace in your hearts to the Lord" (Col. 3:16).

So use song. Use it for worshiping God, for praising Him. And use it to teach boys and girls about the Lord Jesus Christ. You can do this from the time they learn *Jesus Loves Me.*

As a wise parent you will provide your family with hymn books. Teach the children sacred songs. Have good times singing together at home. It unites the family in a spiritual bond of fellowship.

If your church is buying new hymnals, you can often buy some for yourself at the same time. Or if not, you can get them through your Christian bookstore. Your family will also enjoy chorus books, especially those with action songs for children.

Discuss the words of hymns. Learn at least one or two stanzas of each. This will bring the message deep into your hearts. It will teach Bible doctrine and will make your family sensitive to the Gospel. Of particular interest will be the stories of how these hymns were written. Such books are found in most Christian bookstores.

If you have a piano the family will enjoy gathering around it and singing a few hymns. Perhaps one of the children can study piano for the expressed purpose of playing for worship. He can concentrate on learning some of the hymns the family enjoys singing.

Music invades the mind simultaneously from four directions: melody, harmony, rhythm and words. It will be tremendously effective in its impact and impression. As G. Stanley Hall has said, "For the average youth there is probably no other such agent for educating the heart to love God, home, country and for cadencing the whole emotional nature, as music."

SACRED RECORDS

"Hi," called Dad as he stepped into the living-room, returning from a hard day's work. "Hi!" he called again. But the children, Johnnie and Sue, were in "another world." They were listening to, "Marching for Jesus," and their little pug noses were almost touching the record as it spun around on their player. Dad smiled. He liked records himself, and he realized that his wife was doing a good job of training the children. She often used sacred records to teach them spiritual truths.

Like the grooves on each disc, sacred songs will penetrate deeply into children's minds because they will be played often and remembered for years.

Young people who are nurtured on great hymns of the faith and on challenging gospel songs, learn to love and appreciate them. Musical "trash" that is so prevalent in the world today, will show up in its true light when compared to these fine sacred songs. Excellent sacred recordings will help to insure your children against cheap, degrading music.

From the time your children are able to crawl, let them hear these splendid sacred recordings. Play them over and over again on your phonograph. Their taste for good music will be developed early. As they grow older, let them start their own record collection. This is one way to invite many outstanding Christian artists into your home to influence your sons and daughters.

RADIO AND TELEVISION

Sandra, a cute five-year-old, had never seen a Christian program on TV. One evening when she was watching, a new Gospel program filled the screen. Suddenly her big brown eyes lighted up. Then she sprang to her feet and dashed to the next room shouting, "Mommie, there's a Jesus program on, a Jesus program on!"

What a pity that children do not have more Christian radio and television programs! They are such effective media, and many secular programs are not fit for adults or children. But there are a few excellent ones that *are* Christ-centered. They readily attract boys and girls and teach them the Gospel.

You may find some of these programs by studying the radio and television log in your newspaper, and by observing notices in Christian periodicals. In time you will locate the Christian programs you want your children to see. During Christmas and Easter seasons there are additional Christian TV programs and broadcasts.

Through the media of Christian radio and television young people are inspired and established in the faith. Too, boys and girls are inspired by the fact that many thousands of others have also placed their faith in Christ.

BOOKS AND MAGAZINES

Freddy looked up, his eyes sparkling like jewels, exhilarated by the trip he had just completed. A pink cloud had taken him over a landscape of alphabetical patches to meet some remarkable people. He had cut through a lush jungle with David Livingstone, he had seen hostile faces become friendly with Hudson Taylor, he had watched the

Indians stalk David Brainerd. He had just finished reading a book of stories about missionaries!

Books can bring to your home great people and noble thoughts. They can mightily influence your children for the Lord Jesus Christ. Giving Christian books that carry simple but moving messages will help shape your children's characters and enlarge their vision. Perhaps a life's work will be suggested to them. As your children read, the ability to express themselves will become easier. For books are to the mind what exercise is to the body.

More than ever before, today's children have an abundance of splendid Christian literature from which to choose. A few Christ-centered books can be found in the secular bookstore, but for most of them you will have to go to your Christian bookstore. There are a number of splendid Bible story books for primary children. These should be in your home and church libraries.

As the child grows older, more books are available. There are even cookbooks which include recipes and devotional thoughts.

Many great Christian leaders have received their vision and inspiration from Christian books. For example, Hudson Taylor, founder of the China Island Mission, was converted by the reading of a tract found in his Christian home. David Livingstone, missionary to Africa, read as he worked as a weaver. That is the reason why it is so vitally important to provide your children with the right literature.

P.S. There's one thing better than a child reading a good Christian book—that is, you, Mom or Dad, reading it *to* him!

"Look, Mom, look," Diana cried happily as she took the Christian magazine from the mail box. She was pleased because she knew it contained several stories for her.

The Christ-centered story is different from the usual "be-good" story. Your children need literature that draws them to Christ. A number of adult Christian magazines have a section specifically for children with stories, puzzles, poems, cartoons, and other materials. (However, be careful of magazines which have a religious guise, such as those printed by Unity, but which teach or imply that good works will take us to heaven.)

If you subscribe to one or more good Christian periodicals, you'll find your child expectantly looking forward to his copy. If you are unfamiliar with Christian publications, ask your pastor or local Christian bookseller for advice.

Of course, two advantages of subscribing to such magazines are: (1) the variety of articles included, and (2) the importance of their regular monthly impact. Through these magazines, your child will realize that Christianity is something vital—something alive and important today.

Don't let the influence of your Christian periodicals stop with your family. Get them out to your neighbors and their children. Or, give gift subscriptions. So often it has been a Christ-centered article that has brought the glorious Gospel to a hungry heart next door.

CHRISTIAN FILMS

Five blind men were asked to describe an elephant. One touched the legs and said, "It is like a tree trunk." Another explored the ears and said, "It is like a fan." Still another leaned against the beast and said, "It is like a wall." To the one who felt the tusks it seemed like a rake, but the man who felt the trunk, thought that it felt like a snake.

Touch alone is an inadequate means of communication. Vision is better. It has been said, "One picture is better than a thousand words." However, sight alone is not adequate. Have you ever watched TV without the sound turned on? You may have enjoyed the picture but you didn't understand all that was happening.

Sound, too, is necessary for complete understanding, and in films we have both motion and sound, and sometimes color, making a most effective means of communication. More and more churches and Christian organizations are taking advantage of this impressionable medium.

Seeing these films will help influence your child for Christ. Before his eyes, frame upon frame will unfold

Biblical and missionary stories as well as stories of everyday Christian living. This latter type of film is especially helpful. A Christian resolves his problems differently from a non-Christian. And religious films graphically portray solutions in a Christian manner.

Presumably, your church will be showing Christian films from time to time. Encourage your children to see them. Also why not watch the newspapers for notices telling where other Christian organizations and churches will be presenting special films? Arrange for your children to go to see them. If you have a projector, there are fine gospel films which you can rent. Your Bible bookstore can tell you about these. Also, you can find them advertised in various Christian magazines.

Christian films are indeed a wise investment of your children's time!

GAMES

Cotton candy—enjoyable but inconsequential. That's the usual concept of children's games! They are regarded as merely a meaningless pastime used to occupy the child's day.

Actually, children learn much through play. They learn consideration (taking turns); discipline (rules to be followed); and most difficult of all, how to win and how to lose graciously.

These are traits which we as Christian parents like to see developed in our children. Games are one of the easiest and most delightful ways to accomplish this purpose. At your Christian bookstore you can find a variety of games. There are box games, such as the Bible Zoo Game, a game about Bible animals. One Christian publisher lists twenty-eight books of quizzes, and many other games of skill. Too, there are Christ-centered books on fun and games, even an encyclopedia of games.

Many of these puzzles and games will help your children gain valuable Biblical knowledge. Through them, they become familiar with Bible characters. These facts are basic. Before a child can appreciate great literature, he must be able to read, and before he can appreciate the great truths of Scripture, he must have some knowledge of facts. Puzzles and quizzes help sharpen this knowledge.

Do encourage their use in your home. Even children who seem uninterested in Sunday school or church will enjoy games. Fun? Yes, but more than that—they are a means of drawing children closer to the Lord!

PLAYMATES

After a child is six or seven years of age, his parents sometimes feel that they might as well take off for the moon in their son's spacesuit. He seems to be paying more attention to his playmates than he does to Mom and Dad. Research in child psychology bears this out. Between the ages of six and eight, children begin in earnest to take their cues from their playmates.

The parents are left wondering (out loud, but it does no good!) what role they should now assume. May I suggest this: accept the fact that it is normal for children to turn to friends of their own age. Therefore, carefully encourage *Christian* playmates for your sons and daughters. Treat your children's friends as welcome visitors in your home, avoid scolding or punishing your children in the presence of their friends. Let your youngsters visit other Christian families where they may talk about the Lord Jesus, their Sunday school lessons and their individual problems. In so doing, they will learn much about the Christian way of life and will find good companionship. So encourage your David to find his Jonathan!

CHILDREN'S COMMUNITY CLASSES

"Bible class today" read the sign in the window. The children saw it and eagerly came. They heard the stories of Jesus—and believed.

Up and down many streets, in many cities in the United

States, you will find Bible classes in the home; many are under the auspices of the Child Evangelism Fellowship, the Home Bible Class Movement, Joy Clubs, and other organizations. Some are sponsored by individuals who want to help the children in their neighborhood find Christ as their personal Saviour.

If there is no class in your neighborhood, you may want to start one. It will strengthen the Christian life of your own children, help their friends, and perhaps reach some children in the neighborhood who otherwise would not hear the Gospel.

The usual meeting is a simple one: songs, memory verses, and a story, often using a flannelgraph and other visual aids to hold the interest of the children.

Undoubtedly your pastor will be glad to help you start a class. You might look in the telephone book to see if the Child Evangelism Fellowship is listed. If so, the local director will gladly help you. Or, write Box 637, Pacific Palisades, California, for information.

Why not ask a neighbor to work with you? Together you can get supplies from a Christian bookstore to start a class for your children. Other parents have done this and in reaching other children, they have reached their *own*.

CAMPS

"One week at a Christian camp is worth a year in a local church," said one enthusiastic mother. Whether this is strictly true or not, it is a fact that boys and girls are influenced greatly by summer camps. There are throughout the United States, many Christian summer camps as well as conferences that feature a special program for children. Attending one can make a tremendous spiritual impact upon your child.

"Why is this?" you may ask. Because of the overwhelming influence of new environment, mass psychology of agemates, interested (but neutral) counselors, plus a skilled and varied approach! The day-long program, consisting of Bible study, recreation, handwork and special meetings give Christianity a natural "tied-to-life" setting. Living for Christ becomes much more than attending Sunday school. It becomes the natural way of life.

At night, the children gather around the campfire and are given the opportunity to express their Christian experiences. These simple testimonies effect other children more than do most sermons. In addition, camp leaders aim for definite decisions and life commitments. When the child gives a pledge in one of the larger meetings, he is usually followed up by an individual counselor who recommends a Scripture memorization plan.

If you can possibly arrange it, get your child out to a Christian summer camp. It is not expensive—and it may affect his entire life. I have seen hundreds of uninterested children and young people go away to Christian camps. But when they came back they were "new creatures." As one parent said, "They did for Bill in two weeks what I've been *trying to do* for years."

DAILY LIVING

"Love God and obey Him."

"Don't forget to say your prayers."

"Don't say you hate Timmy. We're supposed to love everybody."

"Children obey your parents."

This verbal barrage is sometimes aimed at our children because we want to teach them spiritual truths. But we sometimes wonder if we are doing a good job. Especially when they answer:

"I already said, 'Now I lay me down to sleep.' "

"Okay, I'll love Timmy but I'm not going to let him play with my bike."

Such replies leave us blank. So we sit back, with a question mark in our minds, wondering why the spiritual instruction we give our children seems to be of no avail.

But there are other ways to impart Biblical truths to our children. We can capitalize on everyday happenings by making spiritual application in a natural setting. It may be a broken bike, a bug, a brand new ball or a dolly's dirty dress. With Christ it was bread, seed, salt, candles, vineyards, pearls and the eye of a needle.

Sometimes the answer can be pretty simple, yet satisfy the child as well as increase his faith. After Kathy had been making light chatter for some time, she suddenly asked her father, "Why don't the stars fall down?"

"There are a lot of things we don't understand, Kathy, because we're just human," her father lovingly replied, "but this we do know: God keeps the stars from falling down and He can keep you and me safe too, if we always trust and follow Him."

All parents can find countless opportunities to teach spiritual truths to their children. The point is, you don't want to "preach," but rather to let Christian truths assume a natural place in your daily living. When these illustrations become a part of your child's life, they will have meaning, and "When he is old, he will not depart from it" (Prov. 22:6).

PERSONAL DECISION

Too many Christian parents *suppose* their children are Christians when they actually are not. We all know parents who expect their sons and daughters to act like Christians but much of the time the children don't. Why? Because they aren't saved, they aren't "born again" (John 3:3).

Many times a child's religion and Christian experience is "skin deep." Sometimes it seems to modify his behavior but other times it does not. If the child were saved his Christian behavior would be a natural outgrowth of true regeneration. The Scripture clearly tells us, "Therefore if any man be in Christ, he is a new creature: old things are passed away; behold, all things are become new" (II Cor. 5:17).

It is most important that you deal with your child individually to be certain that he knows Christ as his own personal Saviour. Do this by explaining the gospel story to him from the time he can understand at all. Encourage him to learn Bible verses, or portions of them. For example: Romans 3:23, John 3:16, I Corinthians 15:3, 4 and Romans 10:9, 10. Make the plan of salvation simple, perhaps using the ABC method. "A" for "All have sinned," "B" for "Believe in the Lord Jesus Christ" and "C" for "Confess Him before men." (You'll find these verses in Romans 3:23, Acts 16:31, and Matthew 10:32).

Parents and teachers frequently ask, "How old must a child be before he can be saved?" Actually there is no certain age. It depends upon the individual child—his intelligence, background, instruction and most of all, the working of the Holy Spirit. Unusually bright children are able to understand like those who are two or three years older than they. On the other hand, youngsters who are quite slow in their development may comprehend like those who are younger than they.

One clue to a child's readiness to understand the plan of salvation sufficiently to be saved, is his reading readiness. A careful study of the processes involved in learning to read shows that they are not only difficult, but complex. Reading requires considerable physical development, mental development and background experience. Most boys and girls reach a maturity level sufficient for them to be able to start reading, sometime during the sixth year of life. Some are ready a little earlier, and some a little later.

If a child is mature enough to learn to read, he is usually able to understand his need of the Saviour. Many children are saved before they start school.

Notice this interesting verse of Scripture: "Whosoever shall not receive the kingdom of God as a little child, he shall not enter therein" (Matt. 10:15). In other words, the *ideal* for trusting Christ is not the *adult*, but rather, the *small child*.

Do not discourage your child from accepting the Lord merely because *you* think he is too young. He does not have to understand great depths of theology in order to open his heart to the Saviour. Just as adults do, he will understand more and more about his decision as he grows spiritually.

Be definite by asking him to let the Lord Jesus come into his heart, for "as many as received him, to them gave he power to become the sons of God, even to them that believe on his name" (John 1:12). When he indicates his desire to be saved, pray with him. When he has received Christ as his personal Saviour, review these verses with him, helping him to fully understand his decision.

As the weeks go by, follow up the decision by discussing it with him and by teaching him more Scripture about salvation. When your son or daughter is genuinely saved, he is indwelt by the Holy Spirit and he will have a desire for the things of God. However, don't expect sudden perfection. He is still a child and still *in* this world. When he makes mistakes, teach him to go to the Lord for forgiveness. God has promised, "If we confess our sins, He is faithful and just to forgive us our sins, and to cleanse us from all unrighteousness" (I John 1:9).

It is easy for children to "ride along" on their parent's religious experience and it is dangerous, for when the time comes for them to stand by themselves, they have no real foundation.

The decision must be personal!

EXAMPLE

Gary's mother lay resting on the living room couch. Without realizing it she dozed off while her young son was talking to her. Suddenly she was awakened by his indignant voice, "Now listen, listen to me. When I talk to you, you listen."

It was startling—Gary vigorously tweaking her ears, using the exact tone and words that she had so often used with him. Once again she realized that great responsibility that she and her husband faced in rearing their child—a miniature carbon copy.

Children are influenced. And because each child needs

71

an example, it is important that Christian parents live attractive Christ-honoring lives. There is no influence as great as an inspirational life.

Like many others, I was greatly influenced by my mother. Although she told me about the satisfying life in Christ, she did more. She lived it. She trusted in God and I saw the peace and happiness He gave her. Daily she sought the Lord and He filled her heart with patience and confidence. As I watched these great demonstrations of her walk with Him, it was only natural that I should learn from them.

The same can be true of you and your family. As you look to God for salvation and guidance, He fills your life with wisdom and your children will learn to trust the Saviour.

On the other hand, if you are out of fellowship with Christ—critical, unhappy and discouraged, your children will undoubtedly take on the same characteristics. If a parent's life does not reflect the Lord Jesus Christ, His words will tend to evaporate. They'll have little effect. It does no good to preach "peace" to your children if your own life is a sea of tumult, conflict and upheaval. A life lived in the presence of God is more readily heard, seen and emulated.

These then, are some of the ways to influence boys and girls for Christ. You'll find that it is not the great, dramatic events that count, but the little, day-by-day incidents— right close to where you live.

Change takes place slowly. The total effect of all these influences may not be obvious day by day. Little wonder the tiny child asked her parents: "Since nobody looks very different one day after another, when do babies turn into grownups?" We don't know, but turn they do, because the small unseen changes determine the life. And the same will one day take place in the spiritual life of your children.

Just as a succession of taps creates a sculptured work of art, God will use these various taps of influence to create the form He wants in your children.

You can determine your child's future. And although it

takes time, great will be your reward when you see your children placing their faith in Christ. You will be forever humble and grateful that God's great salvation came to your family and that the instrument He chose was *you!*

INTRODUCTION

In this volume, *How to Tell Your Children About Sex*, Dr. Clyde Narramore offers more than sex instruction. He effectively shows that attitudes are among the most important consideration in wholesome sex education.

Many parents and teachers of yesterday failed to realize the importance of instructing their children in matters of sex. Today's parents, however, have come to realize that wholesome sex education, or the lack of it, affects a person as long as he lives. It affects his attitudes. It colors his life. It helps to determine how he will react to his environment. It determines what kind of a parent he will become.

The development of wholesome attitudes entails more than an understanding of the basic facts of the anatomy and physiology of reproduction. Dr. Narramore presents in this book a much-needed, sound and spiritual treatment. It will guide adults in the important job of providing wholesome sex education at the time when it will do most good for the development of a mature, well-balanced person.

RICHARD A. CROSSE, M.D.
Huntington Memorial Hospital
Pasadena, California

ACKNOWLEDGMENTS

Several people have made important contributions to this book. I wish to express special appreciation to Dr. Richard Crosse, Alice Elliott, Marion Ferguson, Sylvia Locke and Georgiana Walker.

Grateful appreciation is expressed to my wife, Ruth, for her months of planning, research, writing and editing.

CONTENTS

THE MEANING OF SEX

HAVE YOU EVER THOUGHT of the various meanings that people attach to the word "sex"? It signals something different to every person. To one it is sacred and holy. To another it is "terrific." To someone else it may seem sordid, and to yet another it is a silent, "hush-hush" subject.

Sex can also mean confusion, sorrow and embarrassment. Why? There are many reasons. Many of them stem from childhood. Our parents and grandparents may have had somewhat prudish ideas concerning sex. To them the subject was often taboo. So yesterday's children frequently received untruthful and evasive answers. It is not difficult, then, to understand why people who have come from this kind of background may feel uncomfortable and uneasy when their own children ask direct questions.

Alice and John are a fine, sincere young couple who want their children to have a clear, wholesome understanding of sex matters. Yet for them it isn't easy. Even the children's simplest questions make John and Alice blush with embarrassment. John puts it this way: "When I was a boy the word 'sex' wasn't spoken in our home." Alice's background was much the same. So even though they are now adults, it is hard for them to overcome the marks left by their early training. That is why they are uncomfortable when they need to discuss these things with their children.

Here is an interesting fact: We can tell our children how a tree grows—or what makes it snow—or why a car needs gasoline. But to explain about ourselves, how we began, how our bodies function—well, that is 'different. And in a way, it should be. Because "sex" in indeed something special. It is so closely intermingled with our emotions and intense feelings that it would be unnatural and inappropriate to talk about it in the same offhanded manner in which we would the weather.

Yes, sex education includes more than anatomical facts. It takes in attitudes, personal example and manner of living. These impress a child as much or more than facts. And it is fitting that they should.

Most parents have a sincere desire to give their children a good beginning in all phases of life. This includes wholesome attitudes toward sex—a most important part of living.

When your child becomes an adult, what will the word "sex" mean to him? Naturally, that's up to *you*. Your skill in sex education today will determine his feelings tomorrow. You carry the key to his future!

ASK YOURSELF

IT IS HARD to help your children if you need help yourself. That is why it is so important to analyze *your own attitudes*. Your feelings about sex subtly but definitely influence your entire approach. Therefore, it is wise to take a close look at how *you feel*. The following questions are designed to help you evaluate your own attitudes.

1. Do you shy away from the sex questions your children ask?   Yes No
2. Do you think fathers should answer the boys' questions and mothers, the girls'?   Yes No
3. Did (or does) diaper changing and toilet training seem distasteful to you?   Yes No
4. Do you feel that talking to your child about sex matters will cause him to become too curious and lead to experimentation?   Yes No

*It is important to analyze your own attitudes
because they subtly but definitely influence
your child's feelings.*

5. Are you discreet in your conversation about matters of sex?   Yes No

6. Do expressions of affection embarrass you?   Yes No

7. Do you often feel annoyed with the opposite sex?   Yes No

8. Are you ever ashamed of your own interest in sex?   Yes No

9. Do you still have difficulty understanding some of the sexual aspects of your childhood?   Yes No

10. Can you talk rather freely and with ease on matters of sex education?   Yes No

11. Do you think specific terms such as "urine," "penis" and "vagina" should be used in talking to children about their bodies?   Yes No

12. Do you and your mate feel free to discuss your sex problems and relationships?   Yes No

13. Would you prefer giving your child a book on sex rather than talking with him?   Yes No

How do you rate? Are there certain attitudes you need to improve? Although it is not essential to have a perfect score, the answers below are undoubtedly the most desirable ones.

Questions 1-4, 6-9 and 13—No

Questions 5 and 10-12—Yes

WHY TELL YOUR CHILD?

DURING A SERIES of parent meetings at the church, the pastor stressed the importance of Christian sex education. "It is our sacred responsibility," he said, "to help our sons and daughters develop into well-adjusted Christian men and women."

The pastor was right. Christ-centered sex education *is* important and these are some of the basic reasons.

1. Sex education helps a child to wholesomely accept each part of his body and each phase of his growth. It

enables him to discuss physical development without shame and embarrassment.

2. Sex education helps a child to understand and be satisfied with his role in life. Boys grow to be men and fathers. Girls grow to be ladies and mothers.

3. Sex education erases unhealthy curiosity. It takes away the mystery. Children who understand the facts and who know that their parents will truthfully discuss their questions have no cause for worry or concern. They are not attracted to dirty stories and pornographic material. Sex education does not keep children from wanting to know—but it *does* eliminate the need for secretive investigations and unfortunate experiences.

4. Wholesome information guards against serious complexes and maladjustments later on in life. It encourages a child to develop *normal* attitudes. Childhood misinterpretations and fears carry over into adulthood and often produce twisted, abnormal patterns in later life.

5. Sex education with a Christian viewpoint helps a person spiritually. It clears his mind of distracting sex questions. It fosters a deep respect for God and His plan of human development.

6. Sex education builds a child's confidence in his parents. If mothers and fathers are honest and helpful regarding matters of sex, children learn to also trust and confide in them about many other things.

7. Sex education given at home in dignity and authority tends to overcome and nullify the unwholesome information that reaches boys and girls from outside sources.

8. Sex education makes human reproduction clear and wholesome. A child should feel that having children is right. He needs to know, as shown in Genesis 1:24, that God planned for each living creature to bring forth after its kind.

9. Sex education provides a child with sound knowledge and good attitudes which pave the way for him to happily accept new brothers and sisters. New family members are not considered "mysterious intruders."

10. Sex education, while making a child proud of his

own sex, will help him appreciate the attributes and capacities of the opposite sex.

11. Sex education removes many sources of fear. It assures a person of his own capabilities and normalcy.

12. Sex education strengthens a person's self confidence. It helps him feel comfortable and well poised around others. This is true regardless of a person's age.

13. Sex education enables a young person reaching adulthood to make sound, mature decisions about courtship and marriage.

14. Sex education lays the groundwork that helps to build a solid marriage. Young people who enter marriage with mature, wholesome attitudes and understanding are beginning on a sound premise.

15. Sex education prepares a child to later become a parent who can, in turn, comfortably teach his own children. Most parents who find it difficult to discuss sex matters with their children were raised in homes where there was little or no proper sex education.

IS INFORMATION DANGEROUS?

MR. MARTIN WAS a little worried over his wife's direct answers to the questions their children asked about sex. He felt that such frankness might invite trouble. These possibilities loomed in his mind: "Do sex facts shock children? Does sex education cause undue curiosity?"

Mr. Martin is not the only one who wonders about these things. Many adults are concerned about how children may react to sex information. But those who have thought it through realize that wholesome sex education does not shock children. It is a normal part of living. Youngsters accept sex information with a wholesome, matter-of-fact attitude when it is presented naturally and without much ado. Knowing the truth is less disturbing than *not* knowing the facts and wondering what they are.

Another significant fact is that *sex experimentation comes most frequently from a child who is uninformed.* In fact, experimentation is one means of getting information,

Children accept sex information with a wholesome, matter-of-fact attitude when it is presented naturally and without much ado.

Clearly stated answers take away from a child's need for finding out on his own. Children who have a wholesome understanding of human development find it much easier to control themselves. Several research studies show that the typical sex offender usually comes from a home where he has received little or no sex education.

Unwholesome curiosity is *not* the result of sex education. On the contrary, children who know the facts and who realize that their parents are willing to talk with them are less preoccupied with sex matters than are other children who are uninformed. Informed children still have healthy inquisitiveness; they still ask questions—but they direct their questions to their parents.

Naturally, there are some sensible guides in giving sex education to a child. Too much information may bewilder and trouble a child. Some parents unwisely tell all they know. The child is often confused and overstimulated when his sex learning comes in such large doses. Listen to the child's question. Tell him the thing he wants to know. That's probably all he is interested in for the time being. Frank and simple answers are always in order. Then wait patiently for the next question. It may be weeks later before he asks again—but he will.

You can save your child from embarrassment and criticism if you tell him that sex matters are to be discussed *at home*. Explain to him that other parents want to talk to their own children about such things. Let him know that although you, his parents, are willing to discuss any question with him, other adults may not want to do so. Your child will readily accept these few simple rules. And it will keep him from pulling "boners."

WHEN SHOULD SEX EDUCATION BEGIN?

NOT LONG AGO a friend and I were talking about family living. During our conversation he asked, "When do you think parents should start giving their children sex education?"

"Well, Don," I said, "parents are giving their children

some kind of sex education all the time—whether they realize it or not."

Yes, a child's sex education begins the day he is born! You love him, care for him, play with him and laugh with him. When he is hungry you feed him. When he is dirty and wet, you clean him and make him comfortable. Is this sex education? Yes, indirectly it is. Through these loving acts you introduce him to a world of love. You give him his start toward being a warm, friendly person, capable of trusting and loving others.

Your mature, matter-of-fact attitude toward diapers, bathing and toileting shows your child that body functions are normal and right. All of this forms the setting and background for the innocent little questions he asks later on. Even though the child is young, he senses your attitudes and he begins to develop his feelings around yours.

"But," you may ask, "when is the best time to give a child sex information?"

The answer is simple. Tell him when he becomes curious—when he starts to ask questions. This usually begins somewhere between the ages of two and four. By this time your child is talkative and active. The "great big world" looms before him. And he asks questions—about *everything*. Naturally, he is interested in himself—in his own body. And of course he notices the body differences of the people with whom he lives and plays.

Parents often say to me, "Dr. Narramore, do you know of a good book about sex education? Our boy (or girl) is nearly thirteen and we want to tell him the facts of life."

Questions like this would be humorous if they weren't so unfortunate. Evidently these parents do not realize that they have been giving their children sex education for years. The very fact that they have not talked with them tells these children that sex is something to avoid discussing. And, of course, thirteen years of age is much too late to begin. By then, some of the most important and most impressive years of life have already passed.

When a child raises questions, do not put off your discussion until a more "convenient time." If you do, the questions may be forgotten and the time of natural interest will be gone.

Sometimes more is actually involved than the specific question might imply. When parents alert themselves to a child's *interest* and *wonderings* they may discover that the unstated questions need discussing, too.

Some children ask questions surprisingly early. And these first "whys" and "whats" are the outgrowth of a youngster's natural curiosity. A very young child is likely to notice sex differences in his own family. He sees that Mommie looks different from Daddy. If there are sisters and brothers, he soon realizes that little girls are made differently from little boys. "Why?" is a natural question. A simple, honest answer reassures the child that differences are normal—that God made girls one way—boys another, and that both are "right" for them.

Unanswered questions at this time may leave a young child with serious worries. He may think that his sister has lost a part of herself, and that his own penis might disappear. A little later, perhaps at three, four or five a child raises questions about his own beginnings. "Where did I come from?" he asks. "How do babies get born?" As he grows older he may not remember having even asked many of these questions. But the attitudes he picked up from you will remain—possibly a lifetime.

Questions are your cues. When a youngster begins to ask, it is your responsibility (and privilege) to help him understand the God-planned wonders of life!

GUIDES IN SEX EDUCATION

1. *The Environment*—Sex education develops best in a sweet, Christian environment. Not long ago my wife and I visited in the home of a lovely Christian family. It was a pleasant evening. The family atmosphere was just "right"— wholesome and relaxed. I noticed the easy, cordial relationships between the parents and the children. It is this kind of climate that nurtures good sex attitudes.

2. *Examples*—Children unconsciously absorb the atti-

A few basic guides will serve you well.

tudes and feelings of their parents. In other words, a good example is one of the best teachers.

3. *Embarrassment*—Obvious embarrassment on the parent's part can signal the child not to ask questions. Or it may cause him to seek information outside the home—information that is unwholesome and unchristian.

4. *Questions*—Your child's normal curiosity shows up in the form of questions. This is good. He is interested in everything he sees—including himself. And he wants to know the answers.

5. *Birds and Bees*—Children can learn about birth, growth and development from pets. A mother cat with baby kittens, or a mother dog and her puppies are fine demonstrators. However, some parents and teachers talk about animals in order to avoid discussing human beings. But evading an issue never settles it. Children want to know about *people*.

6. *Timing*—As children grow and observe people around them, they naturally become curious. So wait for your cues. It is unwise to rush your child into sex education.

7. *Listening*—Listen attentively to your child so you will know what he is really asking. A parent who both hears and speaks can usually uncover a child's misconceptions.

8. *Why Wait*—*Now* is the time. When a child asks, he is ready to learn. So don't try to divert the youngster's attention. He'll wonder why you don't want to tell him.

9. *Too Much*—Answer your child's questions, but don't go beyond his level of interest or understanding. Too much information confuses the answer.

10. *Relaxed*—A child learns best when he is at ease. It will help if your preface your remarks with, "I'm glad you asked."

11. *No Lectures*—Sex education is not a lecture; it is a process. It begins when a child is tiny and continues until he grows to adulthood. Don't wait until your son or daughter approaches adolescence, then call him in for a lecture on the "facts of life." Rather, talk with him whenever he wants to know.

12. *Attitudes*—Your attitude is just as important as your

answer. Your child may forget what you say, but he will always remember your attitude.

13. *Yourself*—Children can pick up sex information almost anywhere—playmates, adults, books, television, radio and many other places. But the best place to gain wholesome information and healthy attitudes is from *you*. It is *your* responsibility. Don't leave it up to your school or church. Use this privilege *yourself*.

14. *Living*—Sex education is not separate from other areas of life. It should be handled as any other aspect of living. It does not require a "special time" and a "special place." It "grows" with the child and should be learned just as naturally as any other phase of development.

THE RIGHT VOCABULARY!

DURING BABY'S FIRST YEAR he makes many exciting discoveries—his hands, his toes, his hair, his ears. Soon he can identify these parts of his body by name.

Knowing the right names for *all* parts of the body is an important aspect of sex education. The right names may seem difficult, although they may seem that way more often to the parents than to the child. But just as Junior quickly learns elbow, ankle and forehead from hearing the names spoken—so he will learn penis, testicle, buttocks, anus, vulva and vagina if his parents use these terms as they talk with him. The words are not hard to say, and they should be used with accuracy when speaking with a child about his body or when answering his questions.

A youngster needs these words. Asking questions will be easier if he has the words to say what he means. Furthermore, if he learns the correct terms in the beginning, he won't have to relearn them later.

Names for body functions are important, too. Children learn many of them in everyday living. Eating, hearing, digesting, lifting, speaking—these all explain body functions.

We call it sex education when the occasion arises to use words such as urinating or menstruating. It would be easier if these words were easier to say. But since there are no accurate substitutes, it is better for a child to learn the right terms at home.

No doubt your child will use simple words of his own choosing for everyday use. This is all right. But be sure that you use the correct terms often enough for him to know what each word means.

As with all sex matters, it is best to teach a young child that with the exception of asking to go to the bathroom, toilet words and really "personal words" should be used only in his own home or with his own parents. It is an important part of his personality development to learn what is socially acceptable—and what is not.

MODESTY IN YOUNG CHILDREN

THREE-YEAR-OLD Betty was *unusually* quiet. Mother looked out of the kitchen window into the back yard. What she saw made her groan, half in laughter and half in despair! But Betty was perfectly happy. All of her clothes were off—again. And she was holding the garden hose high over her curly head, letting little trickles of water sprinkle down over her chubby little self.

Will she ever have any modesty? her mother wondered. But Betty's mother had no need for worry. Modesty does come.

Just "growing up" and wanting to act like other people will teach this small nudist to be modest. There is no set time when this happens, but sometime between the ages of six and eight a child begins objecting to being seen without his clothes. He wants the bathroom door closed when he is toileting. He closes the door to his room, or jumps into the closet if you come into his room unexpectedly.

You can help your child develop modesty by respecting this new desire for privacy. Encourage other members of the family to let him close doors without teasing him. Explain that he has individual rights, even though he is young.

*Just growing up and wanting to act like
other people will teach a young nudist to
be more modest.*

The development of modesty in a child is not entirely related to his ideas on sex. He becomes modest as he grows conscious of being a separate, real little person—himself! The seven- or eight-year-old enjoys short times of being *apart* or *alone*. He slips away from the family to work on a project; or he closes the door to his room to look over his treasures. He also likes to get into and out of his clothes without anyone around. This means that he is "growing up." It is an important part of his personality development—and it is basic to wholesome modesty.

On the other hand, children are *taught* modesty—both by instruction and by example. It is *not* something that is entirely instinctive. The naked savage does not understand modesty; it is not in his culture. And your children will not understand modesty either—*until they are taught*.

Small children must be told what is proper and what is not. And they must be given reasons for the restrictions placed on them. Tell them *why* they must not dress and undress in front of windows. Tell them *why* they must not do their toileting outside in the yard. Little girls should be told what is "lady-like"—to keep their dresses down. Little boys must learn what is expected of them—to keep their pants up and to keep them fastened. Children can learn that it is "nicer" to whisper when they need to go to the bathroom. They will understand *why* when you explain that this is of no concern to others. There is much that children must learn. And they *will* learn—in time. But it takes patience and repeated instruction on your part. And like other social graces and good manners, it will finally be absorbed.

But it does little good to "preach" modesty if you do not practice it yourself. Many adults are *not* modest, much to their own shame and the embarrassment of others.

Once when a little boy was eating his supper in the kitchen with the baby sitter, his mother, who was going out for the evening, came to kiss him good-by. She was dressed in an ultra modern, low-cut evening gown.

"Where are you going, Mommie?" asked the child.

"To a concert, dear."

The boy looked worried. "But somebody might *see* you!" he said.

And he was right. Modesty begins by example. And we as parents should set that example.

But there is a "happy medium." It is unwise for parents to make *too* much of modesty. As children grow older they naturally develop normal attitudes about propriety. And parents who *overemphasize* modesty only cause their children to gain peculiar and false attitudes about themselves and others.

FAMILY DRESSING AND UNDRESSING

LIVING IN A FAMILY means living close to each other. And it is only natural that there are times when family members see each other dressing and undressing. Although each one has some privacy, occasionally a child will come into a room and find brother or sister, or father or mother not fully dressed. When this does happen, remember that your calm, poised attitude means more than anything else you can possibly say or do. For example, a child may forget what you tell him, but more than likely he will never forget your attitude. Your naturalness and your poise let your child know that the human body which God has created is wholesome and worthy of dignity.

When "Teddy" suddenly comes into a room where either his mother or father is not fully dressed, the parent can say, "Hi, Teddy. I guess I didn't close the door, did I? Would you please hand me my robe?" This takes care of the situation without making the child feel uncomfortable. If you can be at ease it will keep him from becoming embarrassed about his own body. And he will learn to accept himself in a relaxed, wholesome manner.

However, in our society a healthy respect for privacy is important. And although a youngster learns about an adult body from an occasional glimpse of his parents without their clothes, it is not well for a child to be constantly exposed to adults who are not dressed.

Seeing a naked body too frequently may arouse feelings

Your naturalness and poise let your child know that the human body which God has created is wholesome and worthy of dignity.

and emotions too strong for a child to cope with—feelings beyond his understanding. It is good to plan your living with a fair amount of privacy—but with a willingness to accept any family intrusion with a matter-of-fact attitude.

CURIOSITY

CURIOSITY IS THE very beginning of learning. Parents are pleased when children want to see ... to touch ... to taste. "Look again," they say, holding little Johnny a bit closer.

And he looks—because a child's curiosity is unlimited. He wants to know about the world around him. He wants to know about himself—and naturally, he wants to know about matters of sex, too. Youngsters know how their own bodies look. But they wonder about others: "Are other children made like I am? What do bigger people look like?"

How can such curiosity be handled in a way that will help a child to learn and at the same time keep his behavior socially acceptable? Children are as *wholesomely* curious about sex as they are about airplanes, animals and boats. Their curiosity about their bodies is normal and natural. And when parents realize this they find it easy to help their children.

Families with both boys and girls have many natural ways in which the children can be brought together. Toileting, bathing and dressing are normal times to see and learn. Wise parents do not keep children apart because they are inquisitive; rather, they provide wholesome, supervised *together-times* to satisfy young curiosities.

I remember Mr. and Mrs. "Smith" who handled their little boy's curiosity most unwisely. His first grade teacher reported that Jimmie had been overly interested in the little girls. Several times he had "peeked" in the rest-room and had tried to get one or two of the girls to show him how they looked without panties.

The Smiths were shocked and embarrassed to think their son would behave in such a way. So they asked me

*Children are as wholesomely curious about sex
as they are about airplanes, animals and boats.*

to visit their home and discuss Jimmie's problem with them. When I did, their *own* attitudes came to light.

"Well, Dr. Narramore," Mrs. Smith said with alarm, "I don't know what makes Jimmie act the way he does. Why, even at home when I change his baby sister's diapers, he wants to see what's going on."

"Have you ever let him see?" I asked.

"Of course not," she replied. "Whenever I change her diapers or give her a bath I always lock the door so he can't get in!"

This, of course, was *not* the solution. If Jimmie had seen his little sister being bathed and changed, his curiosity would have been satisfied and he probably would not have resorted to such objectionable behavior at school.

But what if there is no sister or brother? There are still other ways. Try visiting a relative or a neighbor who has a baby. Just the everyday bath and routine diaper changing will give your child an opportunity to see another body, and to gain knowledge through seeing.

Some parents occasionally let their own dressing time, toilet time, or bath provide the opportunity for the youngsters to see an adult undressed. If you can comfortably do this at one time or another it will give your child a chance to satisfy his curiosity in a perfectly natural way.

However, you may be surprised! Your child may not seem to notice—or he may walk into the bathroom talking about the new slide on the playground, or about the cut on his knee. In your eagerness to help your child learn, remember: Sex is only one of the many interests in his busy mind!

CHILDREN'S EARLY QUESTIONS

CHILDREN HAVE BOUNDLESS CURIOSITIES! They want to know about everything—bugs, stars, water, trains, paint, mud, worms—and a child also wants to know about himself.

"What's that?" a small child asks, pointing to his genitals. If the small inquirer is a boy, the mother (or father) might answer, "That is your penis. All boys and men have one."

If the questioner is a little girl, you might say, "That is your vulva; all girls and mommies are made that way."

But a child's curiosity does not stop with his own body. "Where is Mary's penis?" young Bub asks, remembering how sister looked when Mommie popped both of them into the bathtub last night.

Questions concerning basic sex differences must be answered clearly to assure the child that he is made the way he should be. You might say, "Boys and girls are always made differently. God planned it that way. All boys have a penis; girls do not. You are made just the way God wanted you to be."

A child is likely to repeat questions concerning sex differences. Be patient. If a youngster repeats a question, he simply needs to hear the answer again.

The child may be only three or four when he starts wondering about his beginnings. His reasoning powers are beginning to develop. He remembers the day he went with Daddy to the pet shop and bought their wiggly puppy. On another day he was with Susie and her mother when they stopped in the dime store to get a goldfish. "Mommie," he asks, "Where did you get me?"

Your answer is important. And it must be truthful. In time there will be many more questions related to babies and sex.

Truthful answers to these first questions build a happy and firm foundation for future information. The stork story, or some other evasive untruth can only lead to mistrust and doubt. Sooner or later your child will learn that you have not dealt with him honestly.

"Where did I come from?" the three-year-old asks.

Mother smiles. "You grew right inside of mother's body, and when you were big enough you were born."

"Tell me some more, Mommie," he may say. So you repeat it.

He may not fully understand, but he feels happy and satisfied. Soon he will ask other questions.

"How do babies get out?" This question may or may not

arise at the same time a youngster asks where babies come from. You can tell your child, "Babies come out of a special opening in the mother's body. It is between the upper part of her legs."

Children are often confused and do not understand that in a girl or a woman there are two different openings. It is helpful if you explain, when it seems natural to do so, that in front of the vagina is another opening for urination. It is called the urethra.

"Does it hurt to have a baby?" Be truthful, but cheerful. "It may hurt some, but a mother is so happy to see her new baby that she soon forgets any pain. Doctors know how to make mothers comfortable. Mothers go to the hospital when babies are born because they need extra care, not because they are sick."

"Do daddies have babies inside of them, too?"

"No, only mommies do. God did not make any place in a man's body for a baby to grow. That's the way God planned it."

"Will I have a baby?" Most children, both boys and girls, ask this. Tell them, "Yes, when you grow up and get married you can have babies." Help small boys to realize that they will be daddies, that they will work and care for the mother and the children.

HOW MUCH SHOULD A CHILD BE TOLD?

YOU HAVE HEARD the old saying, "Things are seldom what they seem." In a sense, questions about sex are not always what *they* seem. For example, when little Johnnie asked his parents where he came from, he did not have the slightest thought about sex. He had heard the other children tell which state they were born in and he merely wanted to get his own birthplace straight. "Was it Kansas or Missouri?"

It is possible to tell your child too much about sex—more than he really wants to know. This is why *listening* is as important as explaining.

Listen carefully to what your child asks. Fortunately he

does not want or need a lengthy, technical lecture. Furthermore, a simple, honest answer is more easily understood.

You can easily tell when a youngster's curiosity is satisfied. If there are no more questions—if he starts looking for his baseball—or if he asks for a peanut butter sandwich, you can be sure he has all of the information he wants or needs just now.

It has been said that an adult can talk about sex for hours, but a small child's interest usually lasts for about thirty seconds! Too much information is bewildering and confusing. It can also stimulate a child's interest too early.

The amount you tell a child depends partly upon his age. Very young children do not understand much about causes, results, and implications. For example, a child of three may ask, "Where do babies come from?"

You might answer, "They grow inside the mother until they are big enough to live in the outside world." To a child approximately four or five years old you might add, "All children come from their parents—from their mother and daddy. Each baby starts as a tiny little baby inside the mother. Then it grows and grows until it is big enough to live outside the mother."

As a child grows older he will ask more about the same questions. *Some parents make the mistake of reading their own adult understanding into the child's question.* But to go too deeply into this is neither wise nor necessary.

LEARNING FROM NATURE

DEBBIE AND HER MOTHER were over visiting a neighbor lady who asked, "Debbie, would you like to see our baby kittens?"

"Oh, yes," replied Debbie, jumping up and down.

So they went out to the back porch. And there they were! All five little fuzz balls, nestled up to their mommie for a nice warm "lunch."

"But, Mommie," asked Debbie, "what are they doing? Eating their mother?"

Learning from nature is helpful, but it cannot take the place of a child learning about himself.

"No, honey," the mother answered. "They are nursing. You see, when kittens are tiny, they suck warm milk from the mother cat. All babies nurse. God causes the milk to come into the mother's breast so that the babies will have just the food they need. When the babies grow old enough to *drink* instead of suck, they will not need to nurse anymore. Then the mother's milk will go away."

And so Debbie learned how baby kittens nurse from their mother. But she also learned that baby boys and baby girls nurse from their mother or from a nice warm bottle.

Learning from nature is helpful to a child. And children should be encouraged to do so. But *learning from nature never takes the place of a child learning about himself.*

A young child's curiosity begins with his own body, or differences between himself and others. He may also wonder where babies come from. Explanations about birds, bees and flowers do offer a way to avoid direct answers, but they are so remote from the real interest that they may *confuse* rather than *inform*.

An older child is interested and impressed with the intricate ways God planned for the reproduction of plants, insects and all living things. Differences as well as similarities become fascinating information for the inquiring mind of the older preadolescent and the adolescent child. But these understandings need to be based on a wholesome knowledge of human sex facts.

It is not unusual for a child who sees animals mating to also ask questions about people. This give parents an excellent opportunity to point out that like baby colts, calves and other animals, children, too, have both a mother and a father. If a child asks if parents "mate," a mother or father can explain that they *do* but that they are different from animals. Parents can explain that mothers and fathers love each other with all their hearts. That is why they get married and live together—so that they can have a happy family and raise the children whom they love. Such explanations help children understand the mutual and tender love of parents. These explanations also use a natural interest that children have in animals and turn it into wholesome instruction regarding people.

THE NEW BABY BROTHER OR SISTER

GETTING READY FOR a new baby—what a happy time this can be for all the family! And what's more, the anticipation and joy over the expected "newcomer" also offers many splendid opportunities for brothers and sisters to gain a basic understanding of human beginnings. There is much preparation needed to welcome this new member of the family. Layette? Yes, but more than that. Parents should talk over the coming event with the brothers and sisters. Their lives will be affected by the "little one," too.

This is no time for surprises. An unannounced baby can cause misunderstandings and even serious emotional damage. Children must be made ready to accept a new brother or sister.

Bobbie proved this point. A few years ago I was called upon to give psychological help to this five-year-old boy. He refused to speak. Although he had attended kindergarten for several months, he never uttered a word in public.

One day I visited his home. Suspecting that Bobbie had been the victim of a traumatic experience, I asked his parents if he had ever been shocked or terribly frightened.

"Yes," replied the father. "It happened when he was about two years old. That's when his younger brother was born. My wife was about eight months along. I'll never forget that night. She and I had been talking about when we should tell Bobbie that he was to have a new brother or sister. We didn't know just how to go about it, but we decided we would tell him the next morning. Well, the next morning was too late, because that night my wife began to have labor pains and I rushed her to the hospital. Then I dashed back home, picked up Bobbie, who was still sleeping, and took him to some friends of mine in a nearby town. Then I went back to the hospital where I spent the night."

*Your child will be more ready to welcome the
new baby if he knows just what to expect.*

"Was it the next morning when Bobbie received the shock?" I asked.

"Yes," he continued. "You see, he never roused from his sleep that night, and when he awoke the next morning my friends said that he screamed violently for several minutes, then became sick. He wasn't acquainted with the people, so he didn't know what had happened to him."

"Has he spoken since that time?"

"No, hardly any. He understands, and hears us, but just won't talk."

After careful diagnosis we worked with Bobbie and within a year he was talking and reacting in a normal fashion.

Bobbie's case is both extreme and unusual. But it illustrates the effect of shock on the human body and on the emotions.

Parents who "surprise" their children with a new baby may not injure them this severely. But they *do* make it difficult for them to fully understand and to accept the newcomer.

"Where did he come from?" "Are they telling me the truth?" "They like him better than they do me." "Why does Mommie want to hold that little baby all of the time?"

These are natural reactions for children who are not sufficiently informed. Such feelings spell trouble for your child, and for the new baby, too. Jealousy and dislike rush to the mind of the youngster who unexpectedly finds a tiny "darling" in his mother's arms.

Parents may think that the other children in the family just naturally know that a baby is coming. "I'm so big!" Mother laughs. "How can they help but know? We talk about it a lot."

But the change comes gradually. And young children may not pay much attention to grown-up conversation. As a result, they may not fully understand. This is good to a certain point, because it is extremely hard for a youngster to have the seemingly endless wait of seven or eight long months. But after a little while, the parents should break the happy news that a new brother or sister is coming to live with them.

Sometimes children do notice that mother is getting larger. "Mommy, you're so fat," says three-year-old Mark. "Mother is a fatty—Mother is a fatty," sings four-year-old Joy.

Now is the time for honesty. "Yes," mother agrees, "I *am* getting bigger. And there's a good reason why Mommie's tummy is getting larger. Let me tell you a very happy secret: A little baby is growing inside of me!" Then as you give the children a little hug, add: "This is just the way I looked when I was waiting for you to be born. I was happy *then* and of course I'm happy now."

Children enjoy getting things ready for the new baby. They like to see the tiny new clothes and they take pride in folding them and putting them away. The more the child is in on the "getting-ready," the more he feels that this is *his* baby too.

If the new baby is going to use the crib now being used by an older child, be sure to make a special occasion of getting the larger bed all ready before you say much about using the crib for the new baby. This will help the older child share happily. In fact, some parents have asked where they should let the new baby sleep. Often the youngest child suggests that the newcomer use *his* crib!

Your youngster will be more ready to welcome the new baby if he knows just what to expect. These are some of the things that a child needs to know:

- We do not know whether the new baby will be a boy or a girl. But we are sure that God will send the one that is *just right* for the family.
- New babies are little. Show him just about how big, about like Susan's doll—so little that they can't play games or talk.
- New babies can't eat grown-up foods. They have no teeth.
- Babies suck to get their food. Mother's breasts will have milk in them when the baby is ready to eat. (Let him know he also nursed.)

— A new baby cries often, but it doesn't mean he is hurt or sick. Crying is his way of talking. He is letting you know that he wants something to eat, or some dry clothes.

— The new baby will sleep much of the time. Babies need lots of sleep to help them grow.

Your child should also know ahead of time that Mother will be going to the hospital. He will be interested in the whole plan: who will stay with him—how long Mother will be gone—how much fun it will be for Mother to come home and see the family again. All of these facts can be woven into a happy bedtime story. And telling it once is not enough. It is a story your child will want you to repeat quite often. When you prepare him in this way, he will be at ease when the time comes for Mother to leave for the hospital.

During the time of waiting for the new baby, children ask many things. You can expect questions such as these more than once:

— "Does the baby hurt you?"
— "Is the baby in your stomach now?"
— "How did the baby get inside?"
— "How is the baby going to get out?"
— "Is it going to hurt you when the baby comes out?"

The age and the understanding of your child will tell you how much information is needed to satisfactorily answer his questions. Be truthful, keeping in mind that each basic fact will strengthen your child's understanding. Smile as you answer. Be happy and make the little questioner comfortable and happy. Remember: Your wholesome, Christian attitude toward sex will become his! You may have to repeat things you thought he clearly grasped, but these repetitions are important—someday he will fit all of the pieces of information together and *really* understand!

WHEN CHILDREN SHARE INFORMATION

AFTER A BIBLE STORY and bedtime prayers, Mother tucked Janie in for the night. Just as Mother was ready to leave the room, Janie propped herself up on one elbow and said, "Mother, do you know what? Linda says her mother is going to have a baby. She even told me how it was going to be born."

Janie's mother felt a waver of uncertainty. *Should children be talking about such things?* she wondered.

Parents are often alarmed when they learn that their children have been "talking things over." But one thing is certain: Some such talk among children is inevitable, and not all of the childish exchange of information is bad or unwholesome. In many cases it is of real value—because children explain things to each other in a natural, easy manner and in language they understand.

If you have a friendly, relaxed relationship with your children, built on years of working things out together, you can expect them to bring bits of picked up information for you to explain. This is an invaluable opportunity: a time for you to correct mistaken ideas, a time for you to minimize anxieties and a chance to explain things further.

What should parents do when children share sex information? Because of the nature of sex, children *do* need guidance. Be sure your child knows that most parents want to tell their *own* youngsters about sex matters. Explain that you, too, prefer that questions and ideas about sex be discussed *at home*. Help him understand that there are many times when a conversation about sex is out of place—that these subjects are usually discussed just in the privacy of the family.

Children need to learn what is acceptable and what is not. Naturally, young children do not know what is appropriate unless you tell them. It is your responsibility to quietly explain *why* we talk about sex matters in a discreet manner. Such instruction not only teaches a child to be more acceptable during his formative years; it also helps him to be discreet when he becomes an adult. We all know grownups who are shunned because they have never learned that sex matters are personal—not to be glibly spoken about like the weather.

When children share sex information, you have at least two responsibilities: (1) Explain to your child why we do

In many cases, childhood sharing of information may have real value because children explain things to each other in a natural, easy manner and in language they understand.

not discuss personal matters out of the home, and (2) explain to your child that the boy or girl who continually talks about sex is not using good manners and probably does not have the right information anyway. Assure your child that you will be glad to talk with him (or her) about personal matters anytime he wants to.

EXPERIMENTATION

ON A NUMBER of occasions, school officials have asked me to assist them in working with parents on problems concerning sex play among small children. Although most of these incidents have taken place in the neighborhood and not at school, disturbed parents have reported the occurrence to school principals and teachers, asking that their child not be permitted "to play with such children."

Many mothers and fathers have been shocked and upset to find a group of neighborhood children involved in sex play. But there is no real need for panic. Sex play and experimentation are not at all uncommon among children between the ages of four to ten.

Youngsters want to compare, to find out. So behind closed doors they show each other their buttocks and genitals. They experiment with different ways to urinate. Girls stand up—boys sit down. They giggle about toilet activities and bathroom words. Sometimes their play is more subtle—and they play operation, doctor and nurse. Sometimes it is more extreme—and the child becomes anxious and a bit frightened.

Little girls often play mother. "I have a baby growing inside of me," announces five-year-old Peggy. Little boys have grown up feelings, too. "I'm a fireman," answers Tommy, "and I haven't any time for babies. I've got to put out a fire."

Occasionally, parents are so shocked when they find children have been engaged in sex play that they forbid their child to ever play with the group again. But this is seldom the solution. Such "solitary" punishment may only emphasize the incident and make it stand out unhappily in

Sex play and experimentation are not uncommon among young children. Sometimes it is more subtle —playing "operation," "doctor" and "nurse."

the child's memory as a *dirty* and *bad* experience. Remember: *Wholesome attitudes toward sex are not built on feelings of guilt and shame.*

The best thing you can do is to quietly talk with your child, answer his questions, give explanations and minimize the whole affair.

Wise parents step in and lead children to other activities—without causing a scene. It is not difficult to divert a child's attention if you present him with some new and interesting ideas. Try stimulating interest in other activities by providing some new materials and making a game out of it.

Children must learn what is acceptable behavior. So be loving—but be firm. A definite "no" will put an end to undesirable play. And do not waver or show uncertainty when you say "no." A child *welcomes* definite limits. He feels safe when he knows that his parents are interested enough in him to set up rules.

When you hear of young children experimenting with sex play, you can remember that some of it is a natural part of growing up. On the other hand it might be their way of saying, "We have questions in our minds about sex, but no one is giving us wholesome sex education."

SHARING BEDS AND BEDROOMS

"The house is just too small!" is a lament in many homes today. And it is an honest worry because it is difficult to successfully juggle a growing family into two few bedrooms.

Parents wonder, "Should the children share beds or bedrooms?" "How long can the baby sleep in our room?"

Every child should have his own bed. Youngsters who regularly share a bed cannot avoid physical contacts that invite sex play. Although in every child's life there is usually some such play without any harm, invitation to such activities must be avoided whenever possible.

As I counsel with adults who have sex problems, I find that a significant number of them trace their initial sex

*Children who share a bed regularly are subject
to physical contacts that may lead to sex play.*

experiences to times when they slept with brothers and sisters or with relatives or other friends. Sex feelings are real, even to children. And undue stimulation can arouse and awaken sex feelings that are difficult to control. Many well-meaning parents would be surprised if they knew the amount of sex play and masturbation that takes place when children are forced to sleep together.

If it can be managed, brothers and sisters should have separate rooms after the age of five or six. If this is impossible, use your ingenuity to give each child as much privacy as possible. Furniture already in your home can be arranged to give each child an area of his own. Book shelves, chests of drawers and desks make good semi-partitions.

Children should not be required to share a room with their parents. Even little ones become alarmed and afraid when they become aware of the intimacies of their parents. Darkness is no real protection since children have sharp ears and active imaginations. Even if it means a nightly unfolding of the living room sofa, it is well worth the effort to give parents and children the privacy they need.

CHILDREN WHO DO NOT ASK

IT WAS REFRESHMENT TIME following a meeting of the mother's group at church. Two of the ladies were chatting when one said, "What do you tell your children when they ask about sex? Ronnie had been pestering the life out of me lately with all sorts of personal questions. And frankly, I don't know how much I should tell him."

"That's not *my* problem," her friend answered. "Linda never asks *anything*. It worries me a little because she simply never says a word. It isn't natural."

Like Linda, some school age children have never asked about sex. And in a way it is unfortunate because early questions are usually easy ones—easy, but vitally important. Parents who share the basic and simple facts of sex with young children have paved the way for more complex questions later on.

Why are some youngsters so silent? There may be a number of reasons. Their interest may not be stimulated through natural events in family living. The *only* child, that *last* child in the family, or a youngster whose brother or sister is born when he can't remember the event, is not alerted by the "new baby." So his curiosity may be lacking.

Sometimes the child who does not ask about sex is trying to be "good." Perhaps he has picked up the impression that questions about his body are bad. Such a situation develops when the parents are very strict about all behavior. You have heard parents say, "Why did you do that, don't you want to be *good?*" Children who are under constant pressure to be "good" hesitate to ask questions. They are afraid to risk parental disapproval by making a needless mistake.

The child who is overanxious can best be helped by relaxing the pressure. Praise the youngster for his accomplishments—even though they may seem relatively insignificant. Make your rules less rigid; put your child at ease. Plan fun times with him. Be generous with your smiles and affection. When he begins to feel confident and relaxed with you, he will be less afraid to share his curiosity and his questions.

Sometimes the child who does not ask, has already done so—outside the family circle. But he may have been embarrassed or rebuffed. As a result, he does not feel free to raise further questions—*anywhere.*

Children may remain silent for various reasons—known and unknown. But regardless of the reason, children who never ask the usual questions about human reproduction need help just as much as those who do.

There are many ways you can help your child develop normal interests in personal matters. It may be through his pets. Animals provide valuable object lessons. Many children are encouraged to ask about the beginnings of life through the birth of new kittens or puppies, or by observing these "babies" nurse. But although animals are fine, they are not enough. Your child is entitled to understand *himself*. The knowledge he gains from animal life must be transferred so that he will also learn about *human beginnings*.

Sometimes a few well-chosen books will induce good questions. These books do not necessarily need to be ones that you definitely consider as sex education. They can be delightful stories which can easily lead to a conversation about new babies and where they come from. Your librarian can suggest suitable reading materials for your child.

Another "question-raiser" is the new baby himself. So when your friend or neighbor has a newcomer, take your child with you to visit the little one. You need not say anything especially. Just let your child see the tiny new fellow. And don't worry—the wheels of curiosity will soon start to turn. You can help things along by making statements such as, "You were just about that size when you were born."

In other words, be a good teacher. Set the stage so that your child finds himself in a situation where asking questions is a natural sequence.

But suppose your child is old enough to attend school and still isn't asking questions, even when it seems he has every reason to ask. What then? Is it hopeless? No, you can still help him. Try to *sense* his unasked questions. Observe his behavior closely enough so that you know what his interests are. Then start from there.

Sometimes a child's silence does not indicate a lack of interest, but rather, a fear of asking. When a child senses a grownup's embarrassment or a tendency to avoid such subjects, he often gets the idea that he should not raise questions. So he keeps quiet.

But if time goes on and your child never opens the subject himself, you can help him by beginning the discussion in a natural and straightforward way.

"Did you know that Aunt Hazel and Uncle Jim are going to have a baby? You know, when I was very small I wasn't sure just where babies came from. Have you ever wondered, honey? When you were little, what did *you* think?"

Asking a child what he *used* to think may make it easier for him to express his ideas. In this way he won't have to admit what he is thinking now. You can help guide the conversation by saying, "Of course, you and I know that the baby is growing inside Aunt Hazel's body. All babies grow inside their mothers."

There are other ways of approaching the subject, too. As a mother you can choose some quiet, happy time—perhaps after evening prayers—and then say to your child, "I'm so glad we have you. I can remember before you were born. I used to wonder if you would be a little boy or a little girl. But I didn't really care which you were—I was just happy that a baby was growing inside of me. Every time I'd feel you moving around I'd think, 'This baby feels like a nice healthy little fellow.'"

Your loving, relaxed discussion assures your youngster that any questions or ideas he may have are acceptable to you. Let him hear some of the friendly, neighborhood news that mothers and fathers exchange. "Mrs. Benson is at the Memorial Hospital. She has a new baby boy." "Did you know the Johnstons are going to have another baby? Perhaps it will be a girl this time. They already have four boys."

So if your child does not raise the usual questions, use your ingenuity. If you are alert you will soon find many opportunities (and *natural* ones) to encourage him to "talk things over."

TEASING

WHEN DAD ARRIVED HOME from work he noticed his little girl, June, playing in the yard with the neighbor boy who had moved in across the street. An hour later when the family gathered around the supper table Dad came out with, "Well, Junie, who's your new boy friend?"

Children who are continually teased about "boy friends"
or "girl friends" may come to feel strange about playing
and associating with all playmates of the opposite sex.

Uncertain as to just what Dad meant, June squirmed a little and remained silent.

"Come on now," Dad teased, "tell us who your boy friend is. I saw you playing with him this afternoon."

June, half embarrassed, glanced at her mother, then noticed her brothers and sisters giggling as they began to chime in with the chorus: "Junie has a boy friend, Junie has a boy friend."

Teasing about "boy friends" and "girl friends" is quite common—especially among parents who have not thought it through. "Harmless," you say. Yes, in a way. But something all intelligent parents want to consider carefully.

When a child is continually teased about such a playmate, he soon learns to be embarrassed and uncomfortable. It doesn't take much teasing to make him feel ill at ease and strange about playing and associating with *all* playmates of the opposite sex.

When children have been teased, they sometimes say, "I don't like boys," or "I don't like girls." This, of course, hinders comfortable, wholesome feelings toward others. It makes children self-conscious and ill poised. And when such feelings continue, they may seriously color a person's attitude to the extent that as an adult he may have difficulty associating or working with men and women of the opposite sex.

But there is one additional facet to the problem of teasing. It does not build a good relationship between the child and the parent (or other person) who teases him. It throws up a barrier between them. The resentment may be silent, yet strong—and needless.

All in fun? Yes, most teasing is considered a harmless little pastime. But children's feelings are real. And wise parents will consider the consequences. Feeling comfortable and right with children of the opposite sex and maintaining a happy relationship between parents and child, is an integral part of sex education. It should not be ignored.

FACTS ABOUT MASTURBATION

FOR GENERATIONS the very word "masturbation" brought fear and shame. Parents were filled with anxiety when they found their children were involved in what they thought was a shocking and disastrous habit. Children were often frightened and some were even emotionally harmed by the threats of the dreadful results of masturbation. Many of today's parents want the facts. Here are the questions they ask:

Do Many Children Masturbate? Almost all children masturbate to some extent. It is common and natural for children to discover the pleasant sensations which come from pressing against, rubbing or handling the genital organs. In its milder forms, masturbation is not serious and is to be accepted for what is is, a normal part of the growing up experience. Masturbation is most common between the ages of two and six years, and again between the ages of twelve and twenty. However, it may occur at any age.

Why Do Children Masturbate? Many times masturbation is no more than a part of a child's inquisitiveness about his own body. And it usually passes over without any ill effects or difficulties when other interests present themselves to his inquiring mind. On the other hand, some children resort to masturbation in an effort to compensate for a lack of love and affection—something so necessary for the development of healthy minds and bodies. Some children masturbate because they are stimulated by tight clothing. Still others develop the habit during and following chafing and itching of the skin.

What Damage Is Caused by Masturbation? There is *no* evidence that masturbation causes any physical damage other than an occasional local irritation of the genital area. It does not bring on mental illness, weak eyes, insanity or any other frightening result. Mild masturbation in children is not at all abnormal; it does not cause sexual maladjustment, impotence or sterility. It is not homosexuality. The real injury comes from the anxiety and worry it causes the parents—and then, the child.

What Should Parents Do When a Child Masturbates? In order to help children, parents must first recognize masturbation for what it is—a normal part of "growing up." Infrequent acts of masturbation should be ignored. This is not easy to do when one has been taught that masturbation causes all sorts of dreadful things. But try your best to accept the fact that there is no physical basis for being afraid or worried. Your *attitude* will more than likely determine the end results.

DO NOT threaten your child with punishment. Do not embarrass him or condemn him by saying: "People won't like you" ... "such a dirty thing to do!" ... or "nice children don't do that." Do not frighten him by saying that he will get sick or become infected. Do not offer him rewards in order to make him stop masturbating.

DO look at your child's play life. Does he have plenty of physical activity? Does he have companions his own age? Does he have plenty of play time? Does he have appropriate play things—things he can build, push, pull and handle in his own way? If he is older, does he have a hobby—interests outside of the home? Does he feel accepted, loved and appreciated? If you can answer "yes" to most of these questions there is little likelihood that masturbation will ever become a serious problem with your child.

DO look for other possible causes. Do his clothes fit properly? Is his body clean? Does he have a skin irritation?

Should Parents Talk about Masturbation with Their Children? When a child becomes five or six years old, do not hesitate to talk with him about physically handling himself. It should not turn into a time of embarrassment for him. Simply tell him: "People do not think it looks nice to touch yourself that way. We just don't do it." Let him know that you are not scolding. Be sure that as you discuss it with him, you do it in a calm, relaxed manner. Tell him that all children touch themselves at some time or another, this will help him realize that he is not strange or unusual. Assure him that you know he will not want to do this anymore.

Although "talking it over" may help, it is probably not the best way to control masturbation. If you keep your child occupied and happy, the chances are that the masturbation problem will take care of itself.

What Should Be Done When a Child Masturbates Excessively? Children who masturbate a great deal are usually troubled and unhappy. These are often children who are without friends and who lack a normal amount of childhood fun. In such children masturbation is not the cause of their problem, but the symptom—the warning signal that things are not well in every area of the child's life. So if your child has this problem, check to see what is troubling him. Make a definite effort to create good play situations. Does he enjoy active play? Is he provided with worth-while tasks at home? Above all, is he loved and complimented for his accomplishments? He needs to be included in family projects and family fun. But if after you have completed the whole check list he still does not respond, then it is time to seek professional guidance, preferably from a Christian.

"BAD" LANGUAGE

STEVIE RAN IN the back door with a newly learned word— a really offensive one. Half giggling, he blurted it out and waited for his mother's reaction.

"What do you do at a time like that?" Stevie's mother asks.

To ignore it and behave as though the youngster's word is nothing unusual does not solve the problem. Even a child knows that calm indifference is not a logical reaction. The young offender should know that you realize what he has said. He should know that you understand its meaning. It makes the word less exciting when he discovers you have heard it before!

What should you say? Simply tell him that people consider such language bad manners and unpleasant. Tell him that Jesus does not want him to talk that way. Nothing is ever gained by showing anger or by acting horrified. But youngsters *do* learn from your matter-of-fact disapproval that some expressions are not suitable.

But do not be discouraged if Junior's experimentation with words has reoccurrences—even though you talk with him about it. Trying out bathroom talk, sex words and crude jokes is a stage that many children pass through. However, children who are happy with varied activities usually get bored with such talk before it becomes a problem.

Two-and three-year-olds often repeat toilet words just because they are the ones they know—words they can say with a jingly rhythm. Overlooking them or minimizing them helps these words to disappear. And soon Junior is repeating another "new" word over and over again. And in all probability, this word will be acceptable.

Sometimes a parent may think that a child is being naughty when he says a "bad" word, but actually he may have little or no idea what he has said. Young children learn by mimicking—they add to their vocabulary by repeating new words when they hear them. So if a child picks up an objectionable word from a playmate or a neighbor, it's only natural that he'll try it out for size.

There are several things that can be done to counteract this. Explain to the child in a kind way that some words are not good and we do not say them. Do not make an issue of it because most likely it is not that big an incident to him. Then, as far as possible, check your child's playmates. This is important. Children learn from each other. And it does him no good to be constantly exposed to vulgar language. If he associates with those who talk right, he will talk right, too.

Older children have different reasons for using offensive words and phrases. Sometimes it is a crude attempt at being funny. Occasionally it is a youngster's bid for atten-

HOW TO TELL YOUR

tion. Boys are especially given to using "bad" language. Often, a boy feels it is necessary to know such words and to use them in order to be accepted as a part of the "gang" or to establish himself as a "big shot." Parents can help a youngster at this stage if they will praise him for the acceptable, "grown-up" things he does. But probably the most effective antidote to combat undesirable language is to pray with him about it. When a child learns that such behavior is displeasing to the Lord, it takes on a different meaning. And as you discuss the problem with him, point out what the Bible has to say about such things: "But shun profane and vain babblings: for they will increase unto more ungodliness" (II Tim. 2:16).

HELPING CHILDREN ACCEPT THEIR ROLES

PROPER SEX EDUCATION helps boys to become manly. And it makes girls feel right and happy about being girls. This is important. People often say, "Boys will be boys; and girls will be girls!" But it really isn't that simple. In a sense some boys don't become men and some girls don't become women. They act and react like the opposite sex. Authorities claim that over two million people in America do *not* accept themselves as they are—their sex role. These unfortunate sex deviates were undoubtedly not born that way. Parents, teachers and other adults caused them to turn to unnatural patterns. So it is not enough to "let nature take its course." Guidance into normal sex roles is important.

Although boys and girls *are* different, it is not a clearcut difference that allows us to say, "This is just for boys," and "This is only for girls." Parents who are determined to make their boys out-and-out "he-men" and their girls "real ladies" are on unreasonable territory if they are too rigid in their thinking. Such parents frequently say: "Boys don't play with those things." "That is not a girl's game." "Don't

*It is hard for a child to accept his own sex if
his parents keep wishing he were different.*

be a sissy; boys don't cry." "That's too hard for a girl to do." Statements like these usually tell us more about the parents that they do about the children.

The truth of the matter is that men do cry sometimes, women do enjoy athletics, and although men usually work away from the home, women frequently do, too. Since boys and girls are first of all *people*, they are more alike than they are different. There is much overlapping of masculine and feminine activities. So let your youngster develop his own interests within the wide range of what is acceptable and normal. Your child is a unique person and he needs to grow into the kind of person he really is.

Undoubtedly children benefit from associating with both men and women. Youngsters who associate almost exclusively with one sex are at a disadvantage in knowing what the other is like.

It is unwise to force a child toward an unnatural sex pattern. He should be encouraged to develop into his own normal sex role—without the disapproval or regret of his parents. Francis' parents, for example, longed for a girl. There were already four boys at home. And then the doctor announced, "Another bouncing baby boy!" His parents were disappointed. And they showed their disappointment by often casting Francis into a girl's role. In fact, he soon learned that if he were to live up to his mother's expectations, he would have to play the part of a girl. This was the unfortunate beginning of a long history that finally led to sex deviation.

It is hard for a child to accept his own sex if his parents keep wishing he were different. He finds it difficult being himself. All too often such boys are over-protected, over-dressed and frequently handed a girl's part. And girls who live in such an environment are pressured into male interests, masculine dress and boyish hair styles.

If you want your child to adjust happily to his sex, you should lovingly accept him for what he is. As a psychologist I am occasionally called upon to counsel with homosexuals—adults who are inordinately attracted to their own sex. In nearly every case they have had parents who through the years caused them to be dissatisfied with their own sex.

Parents have the important responsibility of helping a boy feel proudly masculine; of encouraging a little girl to be sweetly feminine. This is best accomplished without undue pressure. In a home where the father fills his God-assigned role as the understanding head of the family, young sons naturally sense their part in the scheme of things-to-come. A mother's loving cooperation as the homemaker sets the stage for a small daughter to find her place. Such God-planned living lays solid foundations for future happiness in human relationships, including marriage.

SHOULD A CHILD BE GIVEN BOOKS ABOUT SEX?

THERE IS AN OLD SAYING, "Books are our best teachers." And of course books are good teachers, but they cannot take the place of a *person*.

A friendly, comfortable conversation that discusses *your youngster's* questions is better than any book. Printed materials give facts, and many of them do it in a natural, positive manner. But it is the author's way, not timed to your child's thinking. A youngster asks his questions when he becomes curious about some particular thing, and it is not easy to use a book to answer what is on a child's mind without getting into other information. And this additional information is often beyond his present curiosity or understanding.

Books are limited in other ways, too. They are impersonal. They cannot create the warm, friendly, wholesome attitude that loving parents can. And this "just right" attitude is one of the most important parts of sex education. In a quiet, subtle way it tells your child that sex is a part of living. He learns to accept it as something that is wholesome and God-given.

Books are important. But they cannot create the friendly, wholesome attitude that loving parents can.

However, there are some parents who find it difficult to talk with their children about matters of sex. When this is true a good book is useful, especially if the parent and the child read the book together. If you are using a book with your youngster, remember to give him plenty of time to say what he thinks and feels. Give him ample opportunity to ask the questions that come to his mind.

Parents can often clarify their own thinking through the aid of a book. It can also be a source where parents can find appropriate answers to the questions their children ask. Your pastor, doctor or librarian can suggest books available in this field. In addition, your Christian bookseller can show you the finest books available.

There are also some excellent books that you can share with your children when a new baby is coming into the family. Written in easy story form, these books help youngsters understand many of the things they need to know about the new baby and the "hows and whys" of his arrival.

As you read books for your own information, as you share books with your child, don't forget: You are the important influence. In years to come it will be *your* actions, *your* feelings and *your* spiritual insights which will take the central position in the attitudes your sons and daughters hold toward sex.

EXPLAINING THE FATHER'S ROLE IN REPRODUCTION

"How DO YOU EXPLAIN the father's role in reproduction?" This is a question nearly all parents ask.

One of the privileges of parenthood is explaining human reproduction to one's children. But the way in which it is presented will affect the children's attitudes for years to come, not only during childhood but also as they enter adolescence, then adulthood. So when parents interpret mating as a wonderful, wholesome process ordained in marriage by God, their children will think of it in the same way.

It is impossible to predict just when a child will ask questions about mating. Each child has his own rate of development. But sometime after five or six, a youngster starts reaching out for greater understandings. He wants to know the reasons why: "What makes my kite fly?" "Why does the cat have whiskers?" "Can fish hear?" There are questions, questions and more questions as he tried to get to the fundamentals, the beginnings. It is only natural for him to ask, "Just how does a baby get started?"

To tell a child about the father's role in reproduction may seem difficult, especially for parents whose childhood training did not include discussion of sex matters. But actually it is easy. And children accept it readily.

Children need to know from the very beginning that every baby has *two* parents. The concept of each baby child and each baby animal having both a mother and a father is important because it paves the way later on for a child to understand the father's part in reproduction. Parents should point out to small children the fact that animals like baby kittens and puppies have both a mother and a father.

When little Judy asks if she can have a baby when she grows up, parents should say, "Yes, when you grow up and get *married* you can have a baby. Each baby needs both a mother and a father."

"It takes a mother and a father to start a baby." This explanation may be enough for awhile, but not for long. In time—possibly between six and nine years of age, the child will want to know just how this comes about. Simply tell him that a cell (or seed, or sperm) from the father must join with a cell (or seed, or egg) in the mother's body. These father and mother cells are so small that you cannot even see them. But after they are joined together, a wonderful thing happens—God causes a baby to start growing. And when the baby has grown big enough, it is born.

Perhaps immediately, perhaps later, your child will ask, "But how does the father's seed get into the mother?"

Then you can say, "You know how a boy is made—he has a penis. You know that a girl is made differently. She has an opening called a vagina. God planned this difference. He made a man different from a woman so it would be possible for a baby to be started. God planned it in such a way that the father's penis can fit into the mother's vagina. The tiny little seed (called semen) flows from the father's penis into the mother. This is the way all babies are started. And it is God's way for a little new life to begin."

It is important that your child know the difference between semen and urine. Explain to him that semen is not urine; it is quite different, and is especially made to carry the sperm from the father's body.

Parents realize that any answer they give their children concerning sexual intercourse leaves much unexplained because a child cannot understand the deep feelings involved. These understandings will come to him as he grows older.

The answers he needs at this time must be ones that make sense when they are added to the facts he has been given before. He needs truthful answers, ones which give the father's role its rightful importance in the family picture.

But be sure that *love* is a vital part of the story. Tell of the love a mother and father have for each other. Speak of the fact that they *want* a baby to love. And of course, actions speak louder than words. Youngsters become capable of receiving and expressing love when they are loved themselves—when their parents create a family life of warmth and affection. And when a child has been reared in an atmosphere of love, he senses the fact that love is an integral part of sex.

It is easy for a child to accept the father's part in the wonderful story of fertilization when his daddy has been a comforter, a story reader and an excursion engineer as well as a disciplinarian. In homes where both parents lovingly work out family problems and plan the family fun, children are quick to say, "Of course we need *two* parents. Daddies are important, and fun, too!"

These, then, are the natural steps in explaining the father's part in reproduction: (1) Every baby has a mother and a father, (2) God has wonderfully planned it this way, (3) Sexual relations are the result of the mother and father loving each other so much, and (4) Give a simple explanation of mating.

WHEN CHILDREN ASK ABOUT MENSTRUATION

CHILDREN MAY ASK ABOUT menstruation at any age. Just leafing through a magazine, or helping with the grocery shopping may make a child wonder about such things. "What is this?" he asks, pointing to a well-advertised box.

Here again your answers must be truthful and also geared to the child's level of understanding. The complex chemistry of menstruation is beyond young children. But they are satisfied with a simple explanation.

Here is an explanation of menstration that is helpful to boys and girls who are approximately nine years of age. Tell the child that while a baby is growing inside of the mother it cannot get its food by eating as we do—so God made it possible for the baby to be fed from the mother's blood. Even when there is no baby growing, a supply of blood collects each month in a special place inside of the mother just to be ready if a baby does start. If no baby begins to grow, then this blood is not needed and it is discharged through the mother's vagina. This happens each month to all grown women. It is called menstruation. It is like bleeding—but not due to a cut or hurt. God made ladies like that; and that's the way they are *supposed* to be. It is part of God's plan to always have fresh blood and proper food ready for a new baby whenever it begins to grow.

"Does it hurt to menstruate?" children want to know.

You can point out that many women do not feel any pain or discomfort at all, while others may feel a little tired and they may not have their usual pep. But almost all women are perfectly able to go right ahead with their everyday activities. As you speak about menstruation be careful to avoid words which suggest pain—like "cramps," "being sick" and "the curse." Such words are unwisely used. When you call menstruation by its right name, you will help your child to know that it is normal and not to be feared.

Sometimes children ask, "Do men menstruate?" Remind your child that menstruation is just the body's way of throwing away blood that is not needed because there is no baby growing inside the mother. Since men never have babies, of course they do not menstruate.

Make certain your girls have a thorough knowledge of the whys and hows of menstruation before they enter their teens. To menstruate without understanding what is taking place can be a frightening experience.

And remember, the process of menstruation is just as important to boys as it is to girls. It gives boys a greater respect for womanhood and it helps them to understand their sisters and mother—as well as girl friends.

THE PREADOLESCENT AND HIS QUESTIONS

"WHAT'S HAPPENED TO JOHNNY?" ask many parents of a ten- or eleven-year-old. They remember the happy, busy Johnny of a year ago, and look with misgivings at the new Johnny. He is often rude, loud and rebellious. He teases and disagrees with almost every adult idea. He doesn't pay attention.

What has happened to Johnny? Nothing too alarming—he's just growing up. And although he isn't exactly enjoyable or lovable during these preadolescent years, he is normal. Most youngsters between nine and thirteen have times of restless, unpredictable behavior as they experiment this way and that way with their many new ideas.

The preadolescent asks many questions similar to those he raised a few years earlier. The clear definite explanations you give him now will help him to become a happy, well poised adult.

Although the new Johnny is hard to live with at times, he is basically the same nice child he was a year or so ago, and he needs understanding and wise guidance in spite of his know-it-all attitude. Fortunately, the preadolescent is a realistic individual, and he is interested in the facts—facts with a touch of the scientific, facts he can check in books. This interest in facts makes him a good subject for sex education—education based on what he cents may want to know:*

Is the preadolescent child interested in sex matters? Sometimes yes, sometimes no. Occasionally it seems that the preadolescent develops a strong and sudden interest in sex. He may try to read everything with a sex flavor that he can find—books, magazine articles and newspaper accounts of criminal sex behavior.

If you have had an easy, friendly relationship with your child during his early years of questionings and all through his year by year development of sex understanding, he will probably come to you with many questions. Some of the questions will seem almost like the questions he asked years ago. Don't make the preadolescent feel self-conscious by saying, "Goodness, I told you that ages ago!" Instead, take the opportunity to give clear, definite explanations. His quick, well-developed mind will have no trouble remembering the terms now. And he will soon fit them into his old understandings of sex matters.

The preadolescent girl wonders—and needs to know:

"When will I menstruate?"

"Why do I have to menstruate anyway?"

"Will I menstruate all my life?"

"What should I do when I begin to menstruate?"

These questions need friendly, correct answers. Menstruation isn't frightening to the girl who understands what it is all about.

A boy has questions, too! He wonders how long it is

*These questions are discussed in the following book by Dr. Narramore: *Life and Love*, Grand Rapids, Michigan: Zondervan Publishing House, 1956.

going to be until he will have to start shaving. He wonders about some of the conversation he hears from certain boys at school. What about girls and menstruation, anyway? If a father and son have had good times and good talks through the growing up years, the boy often feels easier if he can talk these things over with his dad. However, if the mother is handy she may find she is asked questions by either her son or her daughter. Preadolescents may want to know: *

"When do mothers and fathers mate?"

"Does a baby start every time parents mate?"

"How do you know when you are going to have a baby?"

"What does the male sperm look like?"

"Is the female egg like a hen's egg?"

"What makes a baby look like its parents?"

"What makes a baby a boy or a girl?"

"Boys don't menstruate, do they?"

"What is a wet dream?"

"Do people who aren't married have babies?"

Some children have questions but for one reason or another find it difficult to speak about sex matters. If your child is silent don't take for granted that he doesn't wonder. Everyday happenings are good starting places for matter-of-fact information. A family situation, a wedding, a birth or a pregnancy may be a natural opportunity to casually talk things over.

Above all, let your preadolescent child know you love him. Outbursts of temper, arguing and defiance are not unusual with the "almost" grown-up child. Rmember that he is full of uncertainties and much wondering. Give him quiet, firm correction when he warrants it, but also flood him with understanding and love. His confidence in your affection is as important as the information you give him. And it will help him gain wholesome, healthy sex attitudes that will help him become a happy, well poised adult.

SAFEGUARDING YOUR CHILD

MARY AND HER MOTHER were hurrying home from the market. But they had only reached the corner when it started to rain. Just then an automobile pulled alongside the curb, and a friendly sounding man called out, "Want a ride?"

"Oh, uh, well, no thank you," replied Mother. "We'll soon be home. Thank you just the same."

As the car drove down the street, Mary looked up at Mother and said, "Mommie, why didn't you let the man take us home?"

"Come, honey," Mother urged. "Let's walk as fast as we can. It *is* raining hard. And as soon as we get home I'll explain about getting into cars with strangers."

Mary's mother handled the situation wisely. We all know that there is a significant number of criminals, sex fiends and other abnormal people who would take advantage of young children and harm them if they had the opportunity.

From the time boys and girls are quite young, they need to know how to protect themselves from individuals who are potentially dangerous. When you warn children about strangers, you should keep three factors in mind: (1) Do not frighten them, but (2) Do teach them a healthy respect for strangers and (3) Help your children set up some definite safeguards.

You can avoid frightening your child by quietly explaining that most people are good and kind, but some are *not;* and when a person is a stranger you can not always be certain whether he is nice or not.

Here are some rules that you can teach children:

1. Do not go into lonely places by yourself.
2. Do not talk or walk or ride with strangers.
3. Do not stay away from the house after dark.
4. Do not open the door to strangers if you are in the house alone.
5. Do not accept candy or food from strangers.
6. Do tell your mother and father if someone tries to get you to go someplace with him alone.

Try to give these instructions without causing undue fear. However, this is not always easy. Newspapers, magazines, radio and television make sex crimes vivid and frightening to young children. This means that you have the delicate task of reassuring your child that he need not live in fear. "Such cases are unusual," you should tell him. But at the same time it is necessary to make and enforce rules that will protect your child from the "unusual."

One of the most important guides for your child is your own friendly reserve with strangers. Since ideas are "caught" as well as "taught," he will soon develop a natural reserve around strangers—a bearing that will be one of his *best safeguards*.